MW01264807

Stories, parables, anecdotes — these are the transmitters of values, ideals, and even of history in memorable form from generation to generation. One of the best informed and most skillful communicators in this fashion is Jerry Dawson. Hearing him in all kinds of settings, such as conferences, seminars, worship services, committee meetings, and personal conversation, led me to urge him to put this material in print. Although the printed page lacks the Dawson touch of in-person delivery, these pages will enlighten, entertain, and inspire.

A dedicated Christian, the product of Baptist life, Dawson drew his stories from a wide variety of his life experiences. Growing up in a West Texas oil town, he knew first hand the rough, dangerous, and exciting life of the oil patch. Part Native American in his ancestry, he saw life a bit differently (he let me know that "circling the wagons" was not one of his favorite expressions!) than some. In his early years his father was a non-Christian bouncer in a bar who later became a devout Baptist deacon (a person whose company I always enjoyed) and this experience helped Dawson see both sides of church life and understand the profound effect of being born again through faith in Jesus Christ. Dawson's own faith journey began through the witness of a Sunday School teacher from a new church and made him appreciate the need for both Sunday Schools and new churches.

As a young man the molding effect of a Baptist school — Wayland Baptist University (then College) — shaped his life for ministry. His intellectual abilities were stimulated and his devotion to Christ deepened. As a result he pursued graduate studies which culminated in a Ph.D. degree from the University of Texas and began a lifetime involvement in preaching and teaching.

Following God's will to the mission field of higher education he taught history at Wayland Baptist University and Texas A & M University, became Dean of the Graduate

School at Southwest Texas State University, and served as President of East Texas Baptist University before becoming Director of the Christian Education Coordinating Board of the Baptist General Convention of Texas. This later position brought him into constant contact with churches, Baptist schools, and Baptist Student Ministry leaders. He also took part in Partnership Missions in various parts of the world. And interspersed throughout these experiences he has served more than sixty churches as interim pastor. Along the way he became a husband, father, and grandfather — all of which added to his repertoire of stories.

Thus some of his accounts are from the history he knows extraordinarily well. Others are from his own numerous and varied life experiences. His deep devotion to Christ and love of the Bible cause him often to apply the stories to Christian faith and Biblical truth. Readers will laugh and cry. They will gain new insight into the Bible and life. They will come to understand themselves and their world better.

Thank you, Jerry Dawson, for your infectious enthusiasm and for putting in a book that which many have heard first hand — to the benefit of us all.

**William M. Pinson, Jr.**
**Executive Director, Baptist**
**General Convention of Texas**
**Dallas, Texas, March 3, 1997**

---

Dedication

To a VERY patient and long-suffering wife
Margie
who had endured multiple exposures
to the contents of this book and
responded with genuine appreciation on each
and every rendition.

# Contents

# Introduction

My grandfather came to Texas from Missouri with the proceeds from the sale of a farm in a money belt. By the time he got off the train in Amarillo, the Panic of 1907 had set in, which placed him in a highly advantageous state of financial liquidity.

Pap, as the family called him, narrowed his purchase down to two selections: a good farm six miles southwest of Canyon and a big piece of land owned by some folks named Whittenburg.

It should be pointed out that there has never been a good farm six miles southwest of Canyon. It should also be pointed out that his purchase of that other selection could have made me part owner of the *Amarillo Globe News*, KGNC, several banks, and . . . well, a lot!

Whenever the conversation got around to this pivotal decision in the Gibson family history at family reunions, Pap always told the same story.

When he got to Texas he went to work for a while for the Goodnight ranch. The foreman told him that the one thing he must fear above all else was the "blue norther," that fast moving wind-driven cold front that would sweep across the Texas Panhandle without warning, dropping temperatures drastically.

He was told to watch the horizon to the northwest. At the first sign of an approaching storm he must ride as fast as his horse would take him to the barns and safety. It was his only hope for survival.

He was alone on the north edge of the ranch when precisely such a storm appeared on the horizon. True to his instructions, he turned his horse south and rode as hard as the poor beast would run for twenty miles.

Just as he got to the bunkhouse, the storm overtook him with an incredible drop in temperature.

At that moment, his horse fell dead.

Pap said that the back end of the horse died from frostbite and the front end died from heat prostration.

It took me many years to realize that Pap was trying to verbalize for the family the nature of the decision he had made in purchasing the land, and the catastrophic consequences of that decision.

His point seemed to be that it really did not make any difference why the horse died. He died.

And it did not make any difference, in retrospect, as to his decision about which land to buy.

It was easier for him to do it in the form of THE STORY.

After a while I began to realize that every person I met had a story. And it seemed that most folks could relate to stories much easier than lectures, commands, mandates, and orders.

The master teacher of all time was Jesus. The master teller of THE STORY was Jesus. The parable is the ultimate medium of communication.

The key is getting from THE STORY to the truth conveyed by THE STORY.

All of my life I have seen THE STORY in living form. It is my hope that sharing some of these stories may help in understanding and appreciating THE STORY within each of us.

# My Testimony

The most significant moment in my life was when I heard a knock on my front screen door one Saturday morning and opened the door to meet the man who was to introduce me to Jesus Christ. He wore driller's boots, oil splattered coveralls, and a hard hat. He was a tool dresser for Continental Oil Company in Borger, Texas, and I was a lost teenager.

Without so much as a hello, he asked, "Are you Jerry Dawson?"

I replied, "Yes sir."

He said, "My name is Ganelle Brawley. I'll be by to take you to church in the morning at nine-thirty. You be ready."

No explanations, no argument, no excuses, no alternative. And for the second time I said "Yes sir," mainly because he was bigger than I was.

My religious training was virtually non-existent that fateful Saturday morning. There was no spiritual basis for our family, and no effort to include "church" in our life. My Choctaw Indian dad had no interest in church. Besides being a welder, his real pleasure came from working as a floor bouncer in one of the local honky tonks. Mother's religious life was hardly better than my dad's, and she spent a lot of time selling drinks and set-ups at the same dance hall where my dad worked.

Sunday at our home was the day the family spent getting over Saturday night.

You can imagine the problem I had when the local school system permitted the churches of Borger to take a religious census. My sole religious training emerged when

1

I filled in the blank calling for "Religious preference" with the word Baptist. I put Baptist on the card because I could spell it. And the reason I could spell Baptist was because I had seen it on the church sign in front of Calvary Baptist Church, which was two blocks from my house on McGee Street, and I passed the sign on the way to school.

Besides, try writing Presbyterian, or Episcopalian, or Pentecostal. Baptist is easier, and shorter.

Enter at this point a prospective Sunday School teacher who wanted to teach a class made up of young men, and decided to work through the religious census cards to find his prospects. The knock on the door, resulting from the name on the census card, which resulted from the sign on the church, which filled a void caused by a worldly family, was my introduction to the gospel.

I had no idea as to the church I was going to attend, but I made every effort to be presentable at church time.

I somehow knew that you were supposed to wear a tie to church. When my dad learned that I was determined to be ready for my appointment for church, he scrounged around in a closet and found a tie from a distant Christmas, but he had no idea how to tie it.

My only hope was Art, who lived across the alley behind our house. And my faith was well placed, but seemingly futile. Art knew how to tie a tie, but had a typical driller's right hand — he was minus a part of a thumb and had a stiff forefinger. The solution was for me to stand in front of him, and using my good right hand and his good left hand, we tied that church tie.

When Mr. Brawley arrived at nine thirty, he had a car full of young men who were to be part of his new class, and a lasting part of my life. Wayne has gone on to be with the Lord. Marvin has enjoyed a wonderful career in ministry, as has Charley. Garvin is a consistent churchman. Carroll is part of my family.

And in case you are interested, it took a while to fill in the spiritual gaps, but I eventually met the Master between the sink and the hot water heater in the kitchen of Calvary Baptist Church.

As a postscript, one of the greatest joys of my life was the day I preached the ordination message for my dad, as a deacon at Calvary Baptist Church.

# Freedom

My mother was a bright and knowledgeable person who worked hard all of her life at such things as taking in laundry. She paid dearly for it, being ill most of my high school years, and eventually having to spend a year in the TB Sanitarium in San Angelo.

A little past midnight on one of those dreadful nights when we sat up with her in a ward in Northwest Texas Hospital in Amarillo, they brought to the other bed a woman who had passed out at a bar out on Northeast 8th Street.

With my dad working as a bouncer in one of Borger's more reputable "honky tonks," I had had many opportunities to see the end results of alcoholism. This woman was getting pretty close to "end results."

She once had been pretty, but not any more. And over the next couple of days, after she sobered up a bit, it was obvious that she was well educated and had been in the medical profession. (We will call her Annie.)

I finally got to know her well enough to ask her why she was doing this to herself.

This was her answer.

She had been an officer in the nurse's corp in the Philippines when Bataan and Corregidor fell to the Japanese invaders. She was taken to Manila with six other nurses from her group and made to work in the hospital there.

She said that like all caged animals, she and the other nurses planned upon the unlikely possibility that someday they might escape. After years of brutal treatment and abuse while serving in the hospital, the opportunity for escape presented itself in the form of a storm, and their group fled the hospital.

3

Days later, at land's end on the northern tip of Luzon Island, the Japanese finally caught up with their prey.

I shall never forget the look of pure and undiluted hate in her eyes as she told of the decision by the colonel in charge of the detachment to turn the nurses over to the troops.

She was the only nurse to survive the hell that passed in review for them. And she said that the only thing that kept her alive was hatred and a vow to avenge the inhumane cruelty that had been their fate.

She had vowed on their graves that she would kill the Japanese officer who caused it all to happen.

Upon return to Manila, she slowly regained her strength, praying for the day when she might have her moment of justice.

Over a year later, as she worked in the midnight hours in the operating room, they brought in an emergency appendectomy. It was her colonel.

She said she waited until the sentry was on the other side of the operating table. Then she took a scalpel and killed the officer.

The sentry broke her jaw and fractured her skull, and stabbed her with his bayonet, leaving her for dead. In the confusion, her body was spirited out, and she was bandaged and placed in a cast. Again, she asserted that the only thing that kept her alive was her smoldering hatred.

That is how the Rangers found her when they opened the door to her cell.

"Ma'am," said one of them, "you are free to go home."

Annie finished her account by telling me that no one would ever know how it felt when they set her free.

"Oh, Annie," I pleaded. "Can't you see? You are still not free."

*If the son shall make you free, then ye shall be free indeed.*

There is no limit to the evil we can do to one another, and no limit to the good that God can do for us. It is just hard sometimes to get from one to the other.

4

# He Took Our Place

In one of my graduate seminars at the University of Texas in 1956-57, there was a young lady with the now famous numbers on her lower arm. So far as I can recall, she was the only former inmate of a concentration camp whom I came to know personally.

I was struck by the fact that she seemed "haunted" (for want of a better term). She, in turn, seemed intrigued by the fact that I was pastoring a church and working toward a doctorate in intellectual history.

Once, and only once, she lifted the veil behind which she seemed to live, and shared with me her story. But it was not until I actually stood in the wonderful walled city of Rothenburg, myself, that I was able to bring to life in my mind the events she portrayed for me. To this day I have honored her request that I not reveal her identity, so I have called her Elizabeth.

Elizabeth had grown up in a little village adjacent to the medieval city of Rothenburg, in a tight-knit Jewish neighborhood. One of the exceptions to her "managed" friendships was the relationship she developed with a Christian girl she met in Rothenburg outside the Jewish Dance Hall.

Over a period of two years the two met often and shared their dreams and longed for the day when the war would end, and life could be normal again.

Her friend also shared with Elizabeth her faith in God and her belief that Jesus was the Son of God. The willingness to share, and the willingness to listen, created an unusual bond between the two.

They also exchanged fears that "something" might happen to Elizabeth, for the numbers of Jews free to walk the streets were decreasing every day. Elizabeth, in turn, expressed concern about the possibility that harm might come to her friend for being seen with her.

Elizabeth said that one day she was in Rothenburg, and the next day found her in Buchenwald Concentration Camp, to the north of Rothenburg.

A terrible routine of work and separation, of death and hopelessness was finally broken when Elizabeth encountered her friend from Rothenburg. She had been pressed into service as a worker in the camp.

They at least had each other.

Then came the day when her Christian friend came to her bedside in the night and told Elizabeth that the next day they would come to take Elizabeth. Her friend then showed her the numbers she had inscribed on her lower arm. They were Elizabeth's numbers.

Her friend told her that she was ready to die, and Elizabeth was not. They would not look too closely at the numbers.

"Jesus took my place on the cross. Now I will take yours."

The liberation of Buchenwald found only Elizabeth alive. She will not see her friend again until the resurrection.

I never saw Elizabeth again.

I do not know anything else about her life.

I, too, will see her again at the resurrection.

## Deciding What We Are

Dealing with the question of race is a peculiar phenomenon. The nature of our race and the characteristics which seem to go with race are pretty well fixed in us at birth. The social contexts of race are not quite so fixed in us, and are subject to a lot of variables.

My dad gave me life's most valuable lessons about the nature and context of race at age thirteen.

My dad was half Choctaw. We never discussed it much in the family. In fact, in Borger it really did not matter much if you were part "this" or part "that," so long as you could work.

I do remember that I thought everyone in Borger was part Indian. After all, everyone who lived on the lease-land on West Fourth Street between McGee and the city dump seemed to be part Indian, or full blood in many cases. The logic of so many people of Indian blood living in one neighborhood did not sink in until many years later.

My mother was Irish, and I have more of the attributes of her side of the family, but no one could mistake the Indian side of my dad, and certainly not the pure Indian in my grandmother who lived with us for an extended time before her death.

This all helps explain the gravity of the visit to our humble home by a lawyer from the Bureau of Indian Affairs shortly after the death of my grandmother.

The Bureau lawyers all looked alike, dressed in blue $29.00 J.C. Penney suits, flat Panama straw hats, and driving Hudson automobiles.

The Bureau lawyer explained to my parents that recent laws governing Indian tribal relations made it necessary for him to "sign on" or "sign off" the tribal list of the Choctaw Nation. He had to decided whether or not he wished to be under tribal jurisdiction.

In short, my father had placed before him a piece of paper which gave him the power to decide "what he was."

With a sixth-grade education and slow reading skills, plus a deliberate pace for decision making of any kind, my dad asked for the privilege of one night to "think it over," which, of course, was granted.

Though just a kid, I still remember the conversation around the kitchen table that night. My father finally decided that he had always just been a "person." He could not see that being an Indian or not being an Indian would make him more or less than a "person."

As far as I know, it was the only time I ever saw a person actually decide, once and for all, what he was on this earth.

This, of course, is what happens in the life of every Christian convert. This is what Paul talked about when he said in Philippians that our citizenship is heavenly. (*Politeuma — Philippians 3:20*) We sign on or off the heavenly family — forever.

By the way, I still pull for the guys riding around the outside of the circled wagon train.

# Snake Snapping

One of my first "jobs" in the oil fields was that of helping Ace White grab charts.

Gas flow from wells was measured in a little corrugated, steel house built over the pipelines. The meters looked like little LP record players, and the charts made turns and recorded the amount of natural gas produced by an ink line on the chart.

These little meter houses looked forever like a little "out house" and had some peculiar accommodations. Cottonseed hulls were placed on the dirt floor to keep dust to a minimum, and the high compression in the pipelines gave the meter house a very comfortably cool atmosphere, much like an oasis in the middle of a parched desert.

The meter houses attracted the chart grabbers who had to make regular rounds to collect the exchange charts. They also attracted a wonderful array of snakes who happened to like the cool atmosphere and the cotton seed hulls. The fact that chart grabbers and snakes occupied the same territory for even a brief period of time made for some interesting differences of opinion about who had ownership.

Thus enters the assistant chart grabber, whose job it was to deal with the snakes while the grabber dealt with the charts. Standard operating procedures called for the grabber to open the meter house door and for the snake grabber, meaning me, to reach inside and remove the nearly dormant snakes before they got aroused enough to burrow down into the hulls or woke up enough to defend their territory.

My first day, and my first meter house, were memorable. Ace told me to watch him. He reached in, took a three foot rattlesnake by the tail, and popped his head off.

"Did you see that?" he asked.

"Well . . ." I said.

"Here," he said, "I'll show you again." In went the

hand, out came another snake, snap went the snake, and off went the head.

Somehow, I had doubts about the process.

"Let me ask you something, Ace," I said. "What happens if you pop that snake and you don't snap his head off?"

"Well," said Ace White in a moment of clear insight, "in that case, you got yourself one very mad snake on your hands."

My **one day** tour of duty as a snake snapper convinced me that this was not an efficient way to earn a living.

I have since marveled at the vast number of preachers, college presidents, mothers and daddies, principals, bus drivers, trustees, deacons, to name only a few, who try to clear out their meter houses and end up with some angry critters on their hands.

# Dynamite Man

Looking back, it seems like I had several one day jobs in the oil patch around Borger. Sometimes the job only lasted a day but seemed like twenty years. If you think snakes are bad, try dynamite.

Pipelines and dynamite just seem to go together. Blasting was the easiest way to remove rocks from the path of the pipeline. And because of the temporary nature of pipeline work, careless people and pipelines also seem to attract one another.

What bothered you was to have careless folks, pipelines, and dynamite all bunched up together.

That rare combination can make you relish the joys of chart grabbing and snake snapping.

I spent one "holy" day of my life assigned to assist a dynamite man on a pipeline. I call it a "holy" day because so much of it was devoted to prayer and supplication with a mite of repentance thrown in.

His name was Hoppy. The reason they called him that was because he just had one leg. And the reason he had only one leg was because he had blown the other one off with a stick of dynamite.

Be assured, working with a one-legged dynamite man does not inspire a great deal of confidence in your own immediate future. My job was simple. When he set the charge in the hole, I had to help him climb out of the ditch.

His routine was precise. He took out a Barlow knife and cut out a small hole right through the side of the stick of dynamite.

Mercy, I hated to see him do that. Then he crimped a cap onto the fuse, stuck the fuse into the dynamite stick, measured the fuse, marked it off in joints, and then lighted the fuse.

Every time I watch quarterbacks in the NFL with "nervous feet," as certain death bears down on them in the form of outside linebackers, I think about watching Hoppy with that burning fuse and that stick of dynamite in his hand.

He measured the burn and timed it, and snipped off the part still burning. Then he put the charge in the hole, relighted the fuse, and uttered those two words which had already found nurture and life in my heart.

"Let's go!"

You might think that getting a two hundred pound one-legged man out of a six foot ditch is a big task.

NOT SO. All you need is the proper motivation.

What has amazed me since that time is the willingness of so many people to live their lives in that kind of a "crises management" mode. Recognition of the holy power of God should provide enough motivation to get us out of almost any ditch, with enough inspiration left over to move someone else, too.

## What You Wanted

In politics, money often appears to exert an irresistible force on any and all involved in the political process.

For elderly people, time becomes an irresistible force.

For Calvary Baptist Church in Borger, during my senior year in high school, preacher boys seemed to be an irresistible force. Wayne, Marvin, Lanny, Kenny, Charles, Jerry, to name just a few, made up a militant, self-confident, aggressive, and untiring cadre determined to convert as much as possible of Borger, if not the rest of the world, before graduation time sent us on our ways.

The object of our concerted, if not conceited, efforts was a fellow who ran a junkyard over on East Sixth Street. He was one of the tallest young men in town, seemed to be a worthy object of our personal evangelism, and was at least polite enough not to throw us out of his junkyard.

After a blitz of visits, prayer services between the piles of old tires, and absolutely clear descriptions of the bottomless pits of hell (no one knows as much about hell as a high school senior who has felt the call to preach), our  "project" came to church.

At the conclusion of the first service he attended, he made his way to the front, made a profession of faith, and was baptized following the evening service.

Our crew of young ministers-in-waiting were ecstatic. Nothing validates absolute determination like visible results. And this fellow was tall enough to be visible for a long, long ways.

After a couple of weeks, someone noticed that our "project" had not been in church since his conversion and resulting baptism. Since we had memorized the way to his place of business, it was a simple task to load up Wayne's '37 Plymouth and get an appropriate explanation.

I shall never, never, not ever, forget what our "project-turned-product" said when we asked him why he had not been in church since his baptism.

"Look, fellows," he said. "I did what you wanted me to do. Now go away and leave me alone!"

The shame I felt was almost unbearable. The feeling of the moment was compounded by the fact that he never ever made any other visible response to God's call to a full life in Him.

I have been shamed even more to realize how often it is possible to enter projects in His name without so much as a glance to see if He is involved in any way.

## Bud and Believing

Church vocabulary is pretty tricky. Most of the words we use in church have an acquired meaning that goes with an experience. Until you have the experience that lives out the words, you are really using a foreign language.

When I entered Wayland Baptist College as a freshman in 1952, my church vocabulary was very limited. My brief and fast-track experiences as a high schooler helped me build a vocabulary of borrowed experiences, but I had never had to "faith" anything until my first day as a college student.

I had worked in the Borger oil patch on rigs and pipelines, and brought enough money with me to start the year in fairly comfortable fashion, and immediately met my distinct opposite as I started through the grind of registration.

His name was "Bud" and his cause was hopeless.

He had felt the call to preach in Guyman, Oklahoma, settled up with everybody, and set out for Plainview to enroll as a ministerial student at Wayland Baptist College. He had a wife and three children in a 1939 Ford (and two mattresses tied on top), no job, no place to live, and $2.37 in his pocket.

When all of us in the registration line explained to him that he was going to have to produce $175.00 when he got to Red Hardin's cash desk, Bud explained that he had something else in his possession. He had faith that God had led him to this place, and that the financial side of this deal was not "his" problem.

I had never heard anyone say that in my entire life. And drawing upon that vast reservoir of wisdom open to freshmen ministerial students, I took it upon myself to explain that he had to have $175.00, and he had better hope that God also had spoken to Red Hardin about this special arrangement.

The subject was broached about six times during the day of registration and each time it came up, Bud's response was the same — That's not my problem!

Finally, the time came to match vocabulary and experience. There stood Bud and Jerry, and ahead of us were three students and the payout desk.

Enter Billy from Oklahoma. We had gotten to know one another earlier in the registration process, but I was more than surprised when he walked up and said, "Dawson, I have a big problem!"

It was pretty hard for me to generate much sympathy for any problem he might have. His folks farmed an enormous stretch of wheat land in the Oklahoma Panhandle, and there had been some great crops in this part of the world for several years.

"Billy, I wish I had some of your problems," I responded.

"No, seriously," he shot back. "The WMU in my hometown has sent me a ministerial scholarship for $175.00. I don't need the money, but if I send it back, by the time things get straightened out, no one will benefit from it. It is the intent of the WMU to help a preacher boy from Oklahoma. Do you know of anyone who might be able to use this?"

Everyone in line had heard the conversation, and in unison everyone pointed at Bud and exclaimed, "Him, him, him!"

Billy took the check from the WMU, endorsed it with one of the six or seven pens offered to him by the suddenly self-appointed scholarship committee, and handed the check to Bud, who now had proceeded to the front of the line before Red Hardin's desk. He handed the check to Mr. Hardin, who stamped PAID on his bill.

It was when Bud turned and looked at us that vocabulary and experience came together.

"You see," he said. "I told you."

He wasn't surprised. He had faithed it.

# The Tithe And The Tube

Some folks take theological language for granted. Preacher words just kind of float around us and occasionally land on a fertile spot and take root. We eventually use the word and seem to know what it means without going through formal lessons on the subject.

Being raised in a home where there was no "church" language floating around left me with an enormous void when I became a Christian in my high school years. I tried my best to make up for my "church" ignorance, but a lot of the vocabulary never really received a lot of attention, even by the folks who used it.

Tithing was one of those "church" words that I had a hard time with.

I never had a problem about giving money to Calvary Baptist Church, where I came to know the Lord. It was not the most prosperous church in the world and needs were everywhere. And working in the oil fields in the summer, and on concrete gangs on weekends, gave me enough surplus cash to be generous.

Tithing to me was a description of what you did when you gave money to church. It was not a definition of what the giving was.

So, when I felt the call to ministry and got married and left the oil fields of Borger to go to Wayland Baptist College, I carried with me a sweet little wife, a pitiful collection of old furniture, and an abysmal ignorance about church.

Moving from Borger to Plainview was like getting off of a truck and mounting a tricycle. Margie found a part-time job as a clerk in a grocery store and I went to work part-time for Harvest Queen Mills.

Our combined incomes were less than a fourth of what my pay had been as a roughneck!

With all of this in mind, one can imagine how we felt that first Sunday in Plainview when we went to First Baptist Church of Plainview. We seemed to see evidence on every

14

hand of great wealth, and virtually no evidence of any un-met need.

It was a moment of exhilaration.

THEY DIDN'T NEED OUR $2.75!!!

We could keep that meager sum for the needs we had, and when we got to a church that NEEDED the money more than we, we could give it.

It was so simple. And so liberating.

When we got back to our little plywood government surplus 14 X 14 homette after church, I turned on our little green plastic radio we had purchased with Gunn Brothers Thrift Stamps — our sole contact with the outside world.

It blew a tube!

Would anybody care to guess what it cost to replace the tube?

Yep. Two dollars and seventy five cents.

I would never try to tell anyone else what the Lord was trying to say to them if something like that happened. But I can sure tell you what the Lord was saying to me.

He was saying, "Jerry, watch closely. All of this is mine. The tithe is not meant for my benefit, but for yours. I do not need to receive your tithe, but you need to give it."

# Behold, I Stand At The (Back) Door and Knock

When I enrolled as a college student at Wayland I brought with me only a smattering of strong racial feelings.

My formative years in Borger were in an environment that placed more emphasis on what you could do, than your ethnic background.

For instance, I do not ever remember the term "Jew" being used in a negative way. Only in recent years did I learn that one of my friends through my school years was of the Jewish faith.

The student body of our schools included almost every

ethnic and national background one could imagine, except that there were no black students.

Fortunately for me, Calvary Baptist Church had a custom of sharing fifth Sunday evening services with the black Baptist church in town, and I had developed an admiration for the Scottish born Negro preacher who struck me as one of the best trained ministers in the area. Add to this the great gospel quartet he brought with him when we had joint services, and you have just about summed up my experience with black people by the time I entered Wayland Baptist College.

Wayland had already taken a landmark position with regard to integration the year before I arrived in Plainview. Dr. Bill Marshall had led the school to open its door to blacks, not because of some court case or federal mandate, but because it was the right thing to do.

Had it not been for that momentous decision, I would never have known the young lady who was elected by our freshman class as class secretary, or George May, or Bonnell Williams, or Lee from Shreveport.

It was Lee who gave me my very first insight into the awful and ugly nature of racism.

One of the first collegiate organizations to which Margie and I felt attracted was the Volunteer Mission Band, a student-led group of ministry students who produced religious dramas for churches, and scheduled weekend student services all over the Panhandle of Texas and much of eastern New Mexico.

Our mission band team was on the way home one Sunday afternoon, and were overtaken by hunger in Floydada, Texas. A drive-in with a small dining room was about the only thing open to us, all nine of us: eight white people and Lee, a black student from Shreveport, Louisiana.

Lee was the only person I have ever known whose smile was bigger than his body. But he was not smiling as we all started walking toward the door. He said rather apologetically that we should go on in and eat. He would join us later at the car.

When asked what he meant, he said that it would only cause trouble for us to go into the dining room together. He would go "around back" and order there.

No matter what might have transpired through the ages between races to shape the current racial scene in America, one thing was obvious to the eight of us who were free to go in the front door. What Lee was suggesting was wrong!

Without any debate, a unanimous response simply "leaped out" from all of us at the same time. We would all go the back door, order, and eat outside, or we would all go in the front door and eat inside. We tried the backdoor first.

When the owner of the establishment saw us at the back door, he asked the obvious question. Why didn't we come in the front door.

A more thorough look at our group answered the question for him.

We were firm but polite. We were all going to eat together. The location was his choice.

We only hoped he was not embarrassed to have us all standing at the back door.

Then, for good or for bad, he invited us, all of us, to come in and sit down.

I have heard a lot of discussions and sermons and demands and rhetoric about race relations since 1953, but I have yet to learn more about the right and wrong of it all than I did that day at the back door.

## Firsts

"Firsts" are the anchoring points in our lives. The first homer for the ball player. The first kiss from the sweetheart. The first sale for the young salesman. The first weekend pass for the draftee.

Most preachers have a long list of "firsts," such as first sermon, first baptism, first Lord's Supper, first wedding, first funeral.

17

For instance, my first professional presentation, a paper on Friedrich Schleiermacher at the Southern Historical Association in Ashville, North Carolina in October of 1963, is as vivid in my memory as the day I presented it.

My first weekend revival also stands as a unique memory, mainly because it took so long to finish the story.

Our Volunteer Mission Band from Wayland accepted an invitation to conduct a three-day revival at Field, a little church in Eastern New Mexico, not too far from Hobbs. It was to culminate with a dramatic presentation entitled "The Challenge of the Cross."

Saturday afternoon was reserved for a time of personal witnessing, and I was fully prepared to give my testimony, convert the lost, bring in the sheep, and redeem the backslidden all in one mighty effort.

I was taken back a bit when the pastor said that we had only one visit to make that day. This did not strike me as the best use of my very important time and talents.

Then came the great lesson in humility.

It took us almost two hours to get to the sheep ranch where we were to share our faith with a lost sheepherder.

The pastor went to great lengths to warn me that the herder had never spent a night in a house. He had been born and reared in a wagon, had no family, and his sole companion was a sheep dog.

He had been visited by members of the church on a regular basis for at least forty years, and probably had heard more personal testimonies than any man in New Mexico. He would be polite, but he might not say one word while we were there. And most importantly, Jesus loved him.

We finally found the herder's wagon, got out of the pastor's pickup, and sat down next to the smoldering coals of a campfire. After a long while, the herder appeared on horseback, dismounted, and got some tin cups out of the wagon. After pouring each of us a cup of coffee from the pot hanging over the coals, he sat down, nodded to the pastor, and then looked at me.

It was as though he were saying to me, "Okay, you're next. If you have something to say, then say it."

I felt so ashamed of myself. All of the things a nineteen -year-old preacher boy is prepared to say seemed inappropriate at that moment.

All I could do was tell him that only four years ago I had been just like him. I knew that there was a Lord who kept track of both of us — me on an oil lease in Texas, and him on a sheep ranch in New Mexico.

The more I talked, the more I was concerned that I was failing at the most important assignment of my life.

About the time he was convinced I was through, and long before I thought I was, he stood up, tossed the remainder of his coffee into the fire, nodded to the pastor, and mounted his horse and left.

He had not spoken one word the entire time we were there.

We sat there in stony silence a few minutes. I tried to apologize for what I was sure seemed to be a clumsy attempt at sharing the gospel, but he simply waived it off by saying that this was only another page in the book of the herder's life. God would someday finish the story.

The next year Margie and I were on a trip that took us through the vicinity of that church, so we made a diversion and arrived just in time for services.

Nothing had changed. It looked like the same nine or ten cars and pickups were there from the year before. The paint was still showing the blistering effect of New Mexico heat. And the pastorium brought back memories of good fellowship with a pastor who loved his people.

There was one change of significance. The door opened for us as we topped the steps, and the man holding the door for us was the sheepherder!

He still did not say anything. He didn't have to. The joy in his eyes said it for him.

The pastor seemed to sum it all up for us when he said that someone had gone back for the "ten thousand and oneth time." God finished the story.

19

# Lord, Teach Us To Pray

Prayers are seldom memorable, let alone memorizable. It is comforting to know that the Father knows what we are in need of, even before we ask it, and that we are not judged by the eloquence we employ to approach the Throne of Grace

On occasion a prayer is offered that so captures the moment and the imagination that it stays with us forever.

While we were students at Wayland Baptist College, we had the privilege of working with the young people at Aiken Baptist Church some fifteen miles east of Plainview.

The church was a wonderful congregation of irrigation farmers who really believed in the spirit of revival. To say that they focused every fiber of their spiritual being on a week of evangelistic effort is to miss the mark. The week of preaching was almost an anticlimax to a wonderful time of preparation and personal renewal.

So much was the spirit at work in that church the spring of our sophomore year, that the first, and most celebrated, conversion occurred on Sunday morning before the evangelist arrived on Sunday night.

The gentleman who made his profession of faith was pretty well advanced in years, but a babe in the Lord. He was so excited over his new found faith that he could hardly contain himself.

His first impulse was to stand at the door with Bro. Hale, and greet every person who came in as though they were old friends in the Lord.

When the evangelist arrived shortly before the beginning of the first service of the revival that Sunday night, our new Christian greeted him at the door, and proceeded to tell our guest preacher what a wonderful thing it was to walk in the light.

Somehow, the evangelist concluded that this bubbling, joyous saint was one of the pillars of the church, and no sooner had the service started than he stepped to the pulpit and turned to our new convert, and asked him to lead the congregation in prayer for the sermon to follow.

Here was a man who had not been in church long enough to learn the special vocabulary we all assume one needs in order to pray a proper prayer.

Add to that the fact that to the best of everyone's knowledge, he had never spoken in public, let alone in church. Everyone in the congregation knew this except the evangelist.

The only sound that could be heard was the creaking and groaning of the anchor bolts that held the wooden pews to the wooden floor, said creaking and groaning being due to the shaking hands of the man who now had to learn to pray in one simple instant.

After what seemed an eternity, he uttered the most wonderful prayer which consisted of three words.

"Oh, Mr. Jesus."

And that was all he said.

It was all he knew to say.

It was all he needed to say.

Heaven came down to finish what he started, and revival was the result.

*And if I speak with the tongues of men and angels, and have not love . . .*

# The Strings Of Our Hearts

While I was a member of the Volunteer Mission Band at Wayland Baptist College, we made a trip to First Baptist Church, Spearman, for a weekend program. Oscar, one of the most talented men at Wayland went with us to play the violin.

When Oscar began to play, a youngster sitting four rows back on the aisle next to the wall became noticeably agitated. He was near school age, and wore shaded glasses with all the marks of blindness.

The violin music obviously struck a responsive cord with the little guy

As soon as the service was completed, this young fellow made his way down the side aisle, clapping his hands as he walked.

Surely enough, he was blind, and he had learned to navigate by means of sound. His dad was pastor of the church.

He came to me simply because I was the first body in the way. He took hold of my britches' leg and looked up, saying, "Man, can I play your violin?"

My first response was to tell the boy that the violin was not a toy but rather a very, very valuable instrument. But there was such an eager searching in his expression that I took his small hand and led him to Oscar, who was standing next to the piano.

"Oscar," I said, "this young man would like to see your violin."

Oscar was the compassionate person one always knew him to be, and said ever so gently, "Sure, fella. Here." And with that he placed the violin on the piano bench and placed the boy's hand on the strings.

Then the most amazing thing happened. The boy touched a string, plucked it, and then turned to the piano and reached up over the keyboard to strike the correct corresponding note the first try.

I was absolutely amazed. So was Oscar.

The parents then told us of the boy's blindness since birth and the marvelous musical talent he possessed. His mother told of times when the boy would hear a musical rendition, and then come home and reproduce the music on the piano from memory. In fact, there was almost nothing the boy could not do as far as tonal memory, pitch, et cetera, was concerned.

Then a tear come in Mother's eye when she said, "Yes, he has marvelous talent. But we would give it all, and our talents, too, if he could only see."

On the long ride back to Plainview that night, the team reached a unanimous conclusion.

The parents of the blind man healed by Jesus in the Gospel of John could have profited greatly from a visit with this wonderful family.

There is a world of difference between "We would give anything . . ." and "Ask him yourself. He is of age." (*John 9:21*)

## President Dwight Eisenhower

During the early fifties in Texas, drought became a terrible and unrelenting reality. In the spring of 1953 life was almost unbearable, as a series of dust storms blew in from the north and seemed destined to last forever. All of the worst stories about darkness at noonday fall short of the realities of the nightmares of that year.

I stood in the hallway of the second floor of Gates Hall at Wayland Baptist College at 1:00 P.M. during one of the worst dust storms in April, and could not distinguish the lights at the other end of the hall inside the building.

The governors of the states of the Southwest most affected by the spreading drought called a conference in Amarillo, and were honored by the presence of President Dwight D. Eisenhower.

My wife and I were on our way back to Wayland after a trip to Borger. We were stopped for a traffic light on NE Eighth in Amarillo when a motorcycle policeman pulled up beside us and ordered us to "get over! The president is coming."

I immediately moved the car to the curb and watched the cop pull up beside a large flat-bed truck in front of us. The truck was loaded to capacity with a carefully stacked pyramid of thirty-pound Texas Black Diamond watermelons.

When the motorcycle cop yelled to the truck driver the command to "get that ——— ——— thing out of the way,"

23

the driver responded by popping the clutch and jerking the truck right out from under the melons.

About ten huge Black Diamond melons exploded as they hit the pavement, scattering their contents from curb to curb.

Immediately, a motorcade pulled in front of us, and in the back seat of a convertible sat the president of the United States.

His car stopped momentarily as the "mess" was being navigated, with Eisenhower leaning over the side to watch.

Right under Eisenhower's arm, a big chunk of beautiful red watermelon sort of said, "Hey, up there! Take me."

For just a minute, the most boyish grin flickered across Eisenhower's face, and he rose from the seat and extended his arm toward that beckoning chunk of red melon.

Then the moment was gone. The motorcade immediately sped on by, and all that was left was my memory of a melon-loving boy hiding inside a president's body.

## My Own Test of Faith

Nine months after beginning a journey through a world of faith at Wayland in 1952, Margie and I came to what might have been our first serious joint effort at really turning our needs over to a bountiful Heavenly Father.

It was the weekend before finals for the spring term. The money that seemed enough to get us through had pretty well been spent. Margie's job as a checker at Zeiglers Grocery and mine at a mechanic's shop, and our savings from roughnecking the previous year in Borger had almost been enough, but not quite.

I owed $55.00 to the business office at Wayland. I could not take finals until I paid it. In spite of every effort to make our meager funds last, I had no money to pay what I owed.

I had a job waiting in the oil fields the week after finals, but that was of no current value. My mother was in the

TB Hospital in San Angelo, and my folks could not help. For the first time in my life I literally ran out of options and had no way open to meet my obligations.

Margie and I had been working on a part-time basis with the young people at Aiken Baptist Church just east of Plainview. We had learned to love those wonderful people with all of our hearts, and the burden of our debt to Wayland was only made heavier by the fact that we were telling our friends good-bye.

That fateful morning, Margie and I got on our knees, maybe for the first time spiritually, and summoned all of the courage we could muster. It scared us to death to tell our Father that we were going to have to turn our need over to Him.

After this terrifying act of sending our school bill to God, we made our way to Aiken Baptist Church for our last Sunday School hour with our youngsters.

As I walked in the door to the converted school house for services, Clyce Ooley, a deacon at Aiken, walked up to me and almost apologetically explained that the deacons had met for prayer that morning and for some reason had Margie and me on their hearts. He went on to say that he hoped we would not be offended, but they had taken up a love offering for us.

With that brief explanation, he put a roll of bills, tightly wrapped with a rubber band, into my coat pocket and walked away.

I did what any great believing Baptist would have done. I immediately ran to the rest room, locked the door, and counted the money.

There was $50.00 there.

I shall be forever ashamed that my first expression to God was that I had needed $55.00.

As I stepped out of the rest room, I was met by Horace Seago, who said, "Bro. Jerry, I understand that the men took up a little love offering for you this morning. I'm sorry I missed it."

25

With that said, Horace stuck a five dollar bill in my pocket and walked away.

I am not sure, but it seemed at the time that the Lord was saying, "Jerry, you are right. It was $55.00."

# Build Me A Better Preacher
# And The World Will Beat A Path To His Door

My first experience in pastoring a church, if you want to call what I did "pastoring," was at a half time church at Stratton in East Mississippi.

I was absolutely sure that my two years of undergraduate education, and the fact that I was now a tad past twenty years of age certainly qualified me to provide whatever any reasonable congregation might need. That feeling seems to be contagious among young novices. I suppose it is a good thing, because one never really gets "ready" to meet the needs of a church.

The call to the pastorate came from a wonderful little congregation of a couple dozen members who met every Sunday for Sunday School and had preaching on first and third Sundays. A preacher has to possess a high level of self-confidence to think he can significantly impact a church by a one-day visit every two weeks.

On the other hand, churches like that have a built-in immunity to clumsy and inept pastors.

Whatever the balance between the two extremes, I shall never forget their positive and supportive efforts to put up with me.

My reality checks began almost immediately, and not a moment too soon.

Dear Bro. Stewart, speaking on behalf of the committee, explained to me that Stratton had surely seen better days. The timber was gone and the land was pretty poor. The church was reduced in numbers but still felt that they collectively could fulfill a mission calling.

He said that they had become convinced that they could serve the Kingdom by calling young preachers and teaching them all they knew about "church." To be more specific, he pointed out that "we aren't much of a church, but, let's face it, you aren't much of a preacher."

He said they would help me all they could, and one of these days, when I got "good," a better church would put me to work and they would start all over.

True to their word, and in step with their mission, those folks spent the next year trying to mold a rough and inexperienced "preacher boy" into something at least halfway acceptable. Like Paul speaking to Philippi, every memory I have of these sweet people is positive.

I have often wondered since that experience forty years ago and more, if I have been a member who left every preacher in better shape than when I met him.

# Elmer and the Peas

My first pastorate was an experience in inexperience. It is hard to explain to a twenty-year-old "preacher-boy" how little he has to offer a church in the way of leadership. Some churches make the effort to let a young pastor acknowledge his lack of experience and knowledge. Others just wait and watch and giggle a bit while he flounders through the maze.

I was fortunate enough to be called to a little church in east central Mississippi. It was the last part of what had been a neat little rural community devoted to cutting timber, but like so many rural areas devoted to the limber industry, the trees were now all gone and so was most of the town.

The leftovers of both comprised the membership of Stratton Baptist Church, and when the whole bunch got there on Sunday, we counted about thirty folks.

During the entire time I was there, slightly over one

year, the church was true to the mission calling. No church family ever endured pure amateurism with greater grace and more indulgence than did they for me.

Every page of the book of memories I have of Stratton had a learning experience on it. But the single most precious memory I have, had to do with the lesson on the difference between grace and works.

Elmer and Nell were typical of what was left of the former days of Stratton. Elmer had made a pretty good living for himself and his family until both the pine and his health played out about the same time.

After a stroke rendered him immobile, he and Nell just "made do" about the best they could. On Monday mornings before I returned to Mississippi College for classes, my last stop was always at the Tucker house for a visit with Elmer.

Nell would get Elmer to the porch in his neatly ironed Khaki pants and shirt. He would signal recognition with half a smile from a frozen face and a slightly raised index finger on his right hand. That was all he was capable of doing.

We always sat on the porch in wicker chairs. Elmer would listen to me without interruption . . . and sometimes an eye-twinkle . . . for an hour or so, and then I would be on my way.

To say that Nell and Elmer did not have a great deal in the way of this world's possessions is a classic understatement. They did not have much but they were not "poor." Poor is a frame of mind more than it is a state of being, and neither of these two dear folks ever acted "poor." They just didn't have much.

One day as I walked to my car and got in, Nell followed me. When I sat down she leaned over into the window and handed me a small brown paper sack.

"Brother Jerry," she said, "Elmer and I want you to know how much we appreciate your visits. We wanted you to have a little something to show how much we love you."

I opened the sack and found in it a pint jar of Crowder peas. The first thought that crossed my mind was that no two people in the world probably had a greater need for that jar of peas than Nell and Elmer. Even as close to poverty as Margie and I seemed to live while going to school, we seemed well-off compared to them.

I had tried my best in my twenty year old, junior in college theological wisdom to preach the day before on the difference between grace and the law. I must confess that what I had said was pretty "preachy" and not very practical.

It was only when Nell handed me those Crowder peas that I saw the lesson which I have never forgotten.

When Nell handed me that brown paper bag, I was under the law to accept her gift. It was the right thing to do. This was works.

But when Nell offered me the peas, that was grace. Her's was a gift of love and unmerited favor.

## The Lord's Supper or the Last Supper?

The one request made to me at the time I accepted the call to my first half-time church was that we should celebrate the Lord's Supper together as soon as possible. The Stratton church had been pastorless for a number of months, and it seemed appropriate to start a new era in the life of the congregation with this experience.

When I look back upon the comic opera which resulted from their simple request, I wonder what might have happened if I had had a whole month of preparation instead of just two weeks.

I started by purchasing Hobbs' manual for pastors, and practicing, over and over, every step of the ceremony. My one-wife congregation grew very weary of the repeated practice, and I finally had to have "closed practice" to still the harassment from my preacher buddies, but come Sunday, I felt ready.

It started without a hitch. The bread, in the usual offering plate with a napkin in it, was passed out to the congregation and our two ushers had returned to the front.

At that precise moment a family came into the church and sat near the back.

When Bro. Stewart saw them, he picked up "the" plate and made his way to the late-comers.

Not knowing that we were celebrating the Lord's Supper and assuming that we were in the process of taking the morning offering, the gentleman reached for his wallet and removed a dollar bill which he placed in the plate which Bro. Stewart was holding at the man's eye level.

We had not practiced this part.

I had the strangest premonition that I was about to lose control of the service.

The gentleman put his wallet away, folded his arms, and looked up at Bro. Stewart, who in turn looked toward me with an expression that said, "I am about to laugh out loud. Do something."

I looked back with an expression that must have said, "I am about to cry out loud. Do something."

At this point Bro. Stewart lowered the plate and pushed it closer to the gentleman, who was becoming painfully aware that just about all twenty of the people in the congregation were watching him.

So, slowly and deliberately, he reached for his wallet again, retrieved another dollar, and place it on top of the first in the plate. Then he replaced his wallet, refolded his arms, and looked Bro. Stewart in the eye as if to say, "That is it!!!"

I was now absolutely certain that I had lost control of the service.

At this point, Bro. Stewart lowered the place even further and literally pushed it under the nose of our thoroughly embarrassed member.

When he recognized what had happened, he exclaimed, "Oh, my goodness." and grabbed his two dollar bills, one in each hand, which meant he had no way to remove and hold the bread from the plate.

Well, somehow we got beyond that moment, and our perfection before the Lord does not depend upon a clumsy presentation of the elements of the Lord's Supper. The nearly catastrophic part of the experience occurred following the service.

Come to find out, the reason the couple was late for the service to begin with was because they had made special efforts to have lunch prepared for us after church. And Margie had been so preoccupied with our new-born son, who was attending his first church service, that she had not turned around to identify the source of the confusion in the service.

The husband went ahead of us to open the gaps in the barbed wire fences so that we could get to their house for lunch, and his wife rode in the front seat with me and Margie.

At about the third gap, Margie decided it would be nice to strike up a conversation with the wife and began by saying, "Wasn't that the funniest . . ."

She never finished the sentence. While I had little practice with "foot in the mouth" church services, I did have experience in signaling with my elbow when it was time to stop.

I do not remember how she managed to smooth out the conversation, but I do remember that my concern was unnecessary. Our hostess thought the whole experience was pretty funny, too.

The spirit of the church and my love for them grew in spite of, and not because of, a young couple finding their way to service in the kingdom.

I have often wondered if somewhere in Heaven they do not look upon our efforts at "church" and say, "Wasn't that the funniest . . ."

## Set My Soul Afire, Lord

If I thought I was on a high learning curve at Stratton, I was really in for education at my second half time pastorate in North East Mississippi not far from Shannon.

31

The existence of the church was a testimony to the compassionate spirit of Mr. Tom Dunlap.

In the 1930s a collection of very rough men had set up some free enterprise efforts to solve the thirst of the area known as Hell's Half Acre. In the process of defending their territory, three of them got into a knife fight which ended up at the judge's bench with a sentence for each of them to Parchman Prison.

Tom Dunlap had intervened, asking the judge for a sort of deferred adjudication. The ruffians were to be given to him for a year. He would establish a place of worship in the middle of the most incorrigible area of the county, and these three men would serve out a sort of community service sentence. If the judge wanted them back in a year, he could have them.

That became the nucleus for my second church, and those same men were the very heart of the leadership of the congregation, and some of the finest men I have ever known.

In the short time I was with the church, I learned a lot, but nothing else compared with the lesson which began on my second Sunday there. Those fellows hated whiskey. Period. It had almost ruined their lives and they wanted no part of it. Period.

When I parked my car in front of the rural sanctuary, the aforementioned three were standing in a small circle in an obvious state of dismay.

It seems that a bootlegger had set up shop not too far away and was selling whiskey out of a little house he had moved onto a spot where three counties came together. The three men had followed the lawful and legal process of going to the sheriff of each county, only to find that "that fellow had already been there."

Then what?

They had gone to the bootlegger. They explained to him that he had moved that little house onto the property on a truck. He could move it out the same way he moved it in.

Alternatives?

If he did not move it on a truck, he would move it away in a wheelbarrow. His choice, and he had two weeks.

Two weeks later I drove up to the same spot and saw the same three deacons in the same little circle. The only difference was that this time they were laughing.

Sensing that my sermon on love two weeks before must have worked some sort of miracle in their lives, I inquired as to the reason for the dramatic change in behavior.

All three reckoned that their attitude really was inappropriate in the light of the tragedy that occurred in their community the day before.

It seemed that a little house down on the county lines had caught fire and burned to the ground. There wasn't enough left to fill up a good wheelbarrow. Seems like it had been hard to stop the inferno, what with the smell of gasoline all around.

No one ever determined for sure the cause of the fire. There was talk about rival operators who disliked the move he made into their territory.

The only long term effect seemed to be the heightened level of interest I had in the opinions of those deacons at succeeding business sessions of the church.

## A Genuine Mississippi Coon Hunt

Growing up in a rowdy boom town like Borger, Texas meant that there were a lot of things I did that I wished later I had not done. There were also a lot of things I heard about and never had a chance to do . . . and one of those dreamed-of experiences was coon hunting.

You have to have trees to have coons to have coon hunts. And I had built up an almost unbelievable collection of fantasies about coon hunting by the time I transferred to Mississippi College at the beginning of my junior year.

Shortly thereafter, I was called to my first student pastorate in a series of half-time churches, and one of the first notable benefits I gleaned from my power position as a half-time preacher in a rural Mississippi church was an invitation to go coon hunting.

33

"Hey, preacher, ever go coon hunting?" asked Roy.

I told him no, but that I had always wanted to. What did I have to do?

"Tell you what," he said. "I'll come get you at about midnight. I'll bring the 'stuff,' " he assured me.

There began the worst night of my life. He picked me up on schedule. His dogs were in the back of his redford-pickup. I might note that in Mississippi, a pickup does not have to be red or a Ford to be a redfordpickup. Redford-pickup is a frame of mind, not a make or model.

I knew we were in trouble when we got close to the Tombigbee River and the hanging moss started to get tangled in the windshield washers. It was dark. Did I say dark? DARK!

When we stopped, Roy let the dogs out of the red-fordpickup and they dashed off into the darkness, making what seemed to Roy to be an acceptable sound. After a moment he motioned to get back into the redfordpickup and we started up a jungle trail parallel to the river.

Then Roy explained the logic of the coon hunt. The dogs would chase the coon they were after and the coon would head up what he called a "sand spit" in the river bottom.

We would drive up the river for a mile or so, wade out to the sand spit and "cut 'er off." Sounded reasonable to me. Dogs and coon go a mile and a half and we walk a few dozen yards.

Roy handed me a .22 rifle, a set of waders, and a miner's hat with a little light on it. Things were still just fine.

Then we turned on the light on the helmet and looked out across the Tombigbee River.

IT WAS ALIVE!!!

I looked at Roy and at all of those things swimming on the surface of the river and sliding down off of stumps and then I looked back at Roy and said, "Pardner, where are we going?"

Then crazy old Roy pointed out across the water to some sand a few yards away and said, "Right over there."

And then I put on my most manly form of available cowardice and said, "And aren't those . . . ?"

"Yup," he said. "Water moccasins."

"And what if we slid down?" I managed to ask.

"Don't worry," he said with absolute assurance. "YOU WON'T."

It was right after that that I added coon hunting to snake snapping and dynamite work to my list of "once-in-a-lifetime" experiences.

It was not until later in my educational career that I began to see that a lot of folks spent a considerable portion of their lives where even the slightest miscalculation could result in tragedy. The mystery to me to this day is that we would select this as a way of life.

## By These Bones

One of the more interesting sidelights to the ministry of Carlisle Marney was the incredibly talented people who were attracted to his mind.

One of those near-geniuses was the chief forensic expert for the Texas Rangers and the Texas Department of Public Safety. He also doubled as a fabulous scientist-in-teacher's-clothing on Sunday.

I was visiting with Marney outside our classroom one Sunday morning when he walked by, carrying a box of kitchen matches, or so it seemed.

"What'cha got there, bub?" queried Marney, "A fire about to happen?"

The scientist pulled up short, pushed on the end of the match box and slid it open. Inside the box was what looked a little like a calcified chicken drumstick.

He explained that they had found what was believed to be human remains in a creek bed near Laredo, and sent them to his lab for identification.

At that Marney put on his most obnoxious look of disbelief and said in mock sarcasm, "Anybody I know?"

"Well, smarty," he answered, "I feel like it is someone I know."

He went on to say that the remains were probably those of a teenage female, probably white or Hispanic, probably about five feet five inches tall, probably about one hundred and twenty pounds, had poor hair and nails, and was probably born within ten miles of Del Rio.

"In fact, I think I could pick her out of a line-up," he concluded confidently.

I was absolutely amazed, and said so.

His scientific evaluation and his believer's response have never left me.

 "If I can tell this much about a person I have never seen by simply looking at one of her bones, just think how much more God knows about us by looking at our hearts."

## A Personal Invitation from Walter P. Webb

Walter Prescott Webb was a towering presence in and out of his classroom. No other single individual personified better the ideal of the rugged American historian. The nature of the aura surrounding him made it a distinct privilege to be part of his class, and I still treasure the seminar I had under Webb at the University of Texas at Austin.

If there were any unwritten rules for the "campfire atmosphere" of Webb's class, it was that students were neither late nor absent.

Prentis Chunn was pastor of First Baptist Church in San Marcos and enrolled in the seminar. If ever a man fit the description "nasty-nice," Bro. Chunn did. He was the absolute picture of propriety and decorum.

Above all, he was the last person ever to be late for a class.

This helps explain the amazement of Webb and company when Bro. Chunn came puffing into a class already half-spent. Webb looked his way with the look of a sheriff staring at the new card-shark in town.

Chunn offered the explanation none had requested but all were curious about.

He said that he was late because he had been about his duties as a good citizen of Hayes County. Every effort had been exerted on behalf of a bond-issue to build a county hospital in San Marcos.

As he put it, "I have been forced to devote precious hours to overcome the abstinence and obdurance of a bunch of narrow-minded, short-sighted, tight-fisted, redneck ranchers who are opposed to any hint of progress in Hayes County."

With that explanation, the class turned back to the monumental tasks of history.

At the end of the class, Dr. Webb reclaimed the floor and announced, with a straight face and a distinct twinkle in his eye, that it was his custom to host a barbeque for his graduate seminar at his "place."

"I own a ranch about ten miles out of San Marcos in Hayes County," he drying continued.

Class dismissed!!!!!

In the parlance of a class on Texas history, the class wit noted that Bro. Prentis could have sat on a cigarette paper and dangled both legs.

## Oh, For A Tale Twice Told

One of Walter P. Webb's last public appearances was as a speaker for a regional American Heritage Program sponsored by Wayland Baptist College in Plainview. Originally Webb had agreed to speak in February, but he called in the fall and asked to change dates with us so that he could reconcile a date conflict.

It was my privilege to drive to Lubbock and pick up Webb at the airport. As soon as we got past the hello stage, I asked him about the follow-up to the seminar I had taken from him at the University of Texas.

Webb then said that he was in the process of "updating" his view on the impact of the desert core on the West. He always frowned on revisionism, but had come to the place where the term might be used with reference to his basic view of history.

By the time we got to this stage of the discussion, we arrived at Wayland, where a press conference had been arranged. The plan was to have the local station play a tape of the interview during the time slot for our banquet program.

It was my task to get the interview moving, so I began by asking Webb to tell the audience these "new" ideas about the West. At this point I was called out of the room for a while to clarify some arrangements at the restaurant.

When I returned, the interview was about over, and I whisked Webb to the dinner, and then a friend of his took him back to the plane for his return flight.

I then called the station to verify the playing of the tape and to reinforce my earlier request that a copy of the tape be sent as soon as possible.

Disaster! The tape had been erased. Webb's thoughts were gone.

I must have interviewed fifty people the next few days, but I could only catch glimpses and segments of Webb's statements. He was not an "exciting" speaker, and the concepts he had developed and the interview were of little interest to the casual listener. I quickly learned that one tape is worth a thousand recollections.

The greatest disappointment of my professional career as a historian was that Webb's "new point of view" was lost.

Exactly one month later, his voice was stilled forever. He died in an accident almost the hour he originally planned to be in Plainview.

# The Blind Are Made To See

The Lord has a marvelous way of matching your moment of greatest need with His most profound resources. His wells are deepest when we are the thirstiest.

The deepest well of personal influence in my life was Bess Hopper.

After graduation from Mississippi College in 1956, I had accepted a fellowship at the University of Texas and moved in August to Austin to begin my graduate education.

Bracketed around the move to graduate school were the births of our three children—Kim in 1955, Carey in the summer of 1956, and Jamie Lynn in December of 1957. Not a record, but a pretty good showing.

I was called as pastor of First Baptist Church of Mc-Dade in November of 1956, and began the joyful experience of my one and only full-time pastorate.

Any one of the many demands on my time would have been enough to bring stress to a very mature and able person, let alone a twenty-two-year-old university student with a parsonage full of babies.

Within months of trying to set the woods on fire in Mc-Dade, I learned that I could not get a fire started, and the work in Intellectual History at UT was all I could handle. The news of the third addition to the Dawson household was evidently enough to convince one of my deacons, Wallace Wilson, that I had come to the place where I needed some very special help.

"Bro. Jerry," he said, "it's time for you to meet Bess Hopper."

He made the appointment, gave me directions, and sent me on a get-well journey to Knobbs Springs. Elgin, Texas was outside of Austin, McDade was out in the country from Elgin, and Knobbs Springs was at the end of a dirt road outside of McDade. The road went to, but not through, the Knobbs Springs community and Bess lived outside of Knobbs Springs.

I arrived about dark at the modest frame home of Bess Hopper. There were no lights nor any sign of activity except for the distance sound of milk pails banging together in a shed behind the house. I called out for Bess Hopper, and a voice came out of the darkness telling me to "grab the clothesline wire at the front porch and follow it to the shed."

I did as instructed, and ended up in the darkness introducing myself to Bess Hopper as she was finishing the task of milking her herd of goats.

We somehow managed to get me to the house without spilling the pails of milk, and there, when she turned on the lights for my benefit, I saw that she was blind.

She was so delighted to "see" me that she immediately took me to the bedroom to introduce me to her blind, invalid mother and her blind, invalid father, for whom she provided daily care. They were happy people.

We went past a table where Bess was cutting a pattern for a new dress for her mother, and past a bookshelf where some of the books were upside down, the only evidence I saw that there was anything at all out of the ordinary in the house.

Bess sat down across from me and explained to me that before anything else occurred at her house, we should read a word from the Bible and have a prayer, and she immediately opened her Bible to her sighted fingers and read from Psalms 103, and then bowed her head and thanked God for permitting her the joy of having this fine young man in her home.

Then she turned her sightless eyes toward me and said, "Now, Bro. Jerry. What did you come to see me about?"

I had not had one clue as to the reason for my visit with Bess, but the message could not have been plainer if God had sent Moses with a couple of big rocks in his hand.

"You think you got problems, do you? Well, meet Bess Hopper!!! Think problems are an excuse for pity parties? Well, consider my servant, Bess!!!"

I made a lot of visits to Knobbs Springs after that. Bess always thought I came to visit her to make her feel good.

WRONG!

I very selfishly visited Bess Hopper to make ME feel good.

When Paul testified before King Agrippa concerning

40

his life as a missionary, he cited the specific commission he had received from Jesus on the Road to Damascus.

Paul said that he was told to get up and go open people's eyes. He had not been disobedient to this heavenly vision.

I never had the privilege of bringing sight to Bess's eyes, but I can assure the world that being with her certainly brought sight to mine.

Seems like a reasonable test for all of our service.

## Governor Price Daniel

Be careful about your wishes. They may be granted. I spent four adventuresome years, 1956-1960, in residence as a doctoral student and as pastor of First Baptist church of McDade.

I still remember the worst day of those entire four years. I had managed to dislocate a bone in the arch of my foot while playing some sand-lot basketball. My night had been incredibly long and painful.

A young neighbor came over to help mow my grass in a goodwill gesture, but he managed only to sever a water pipe and break the shaft on the mower.

It was that kind of day.

I managed to make an appointment with a bone specialist in Austin; and just as I left the house, a news announcer applied the proverbial last straw when he announced that Price Daniel had just signed a new sales tax into law. That did it!

The sales tax was not a law - it was a personal attack upon me by the governor. I was relatively certain that he had timed it to fit my physical pain as a personal vendetta. My only plea was for fifteen minutes with the governor, so that I could "give him a piece of my mind."

When I got to the medical suite in Austin, the dislocated bone in my foot was almost more than I could bear. Then a fellow came in who looked worse than I did.

41

I had always heard, and preached, that you can always find someone in worse circumstance than yourself, but somehow this magnificent and lofty ideal paled into memory.

Nevertheless, this fellow with a shaggy growth of stubble, blood-shot eyes, uncombed hair and obviously swollen jaw sat down beside, or more like it, behind me. We sat there for fifteen minutes with him telling me about the pain of an abscessed tooth and me telling him about the burden of a throbbing foot.

Then the receptionist made her way over to my poor old, pain-ridden buddy and said, "Governor Daniel, the doctor can see you now."

Like I said, you need to be careful about wishes. I have often wondered if Governor Daniel ever said, "Boy, would I like to have fifteen minutes with Jerry Dawson. Would I ever give him a piece of my mind!" .

## Wallace And The Girls

Show me a church where a pastor is having an outstanding ministry and, given enough time, I can show you at least one outstanding Sunday School teacher who is causing a lot of it to happen.

One of my most memorable revival experiences originated in the dedication of precisely such a teacher.

The preacher for the week was a former missionary recently returned from Africa. The music was outstanding. People were praying. Attendance was exceptional. And nothing was happening.

On Wednesday night, before the beginning of the service, Bro. Wallace Wilson shared with me the conviction he had that three sisters from his Sunday School class were going to accept the Lord that night.

The sisters in question had grown up in the church. They were wonderful young ladies and held in high respect by everyone who knew them. The could be considered "good" by any generally accepted moral code. And they were lost.

When Bro. Wallace shared his belief in that night as a night of victory for those young ladies, I could hardly wait for the invitation time.

At the end of a fine sermon and a wonderful invitation, nothing happened. I was devastated and disappointed, but after an extended invitation, there was nothing to do but have the benediction and go home.

While Buck Walker led in the dismissal prayer, I heard the sound of someone opening the door to my study which was right next to the pulpit. After the prayer I slipped into the study to find Bro. Wallace on his face on the floor, crying for the souls of those three young ladies.

About two in the morning the phone rang. We were on a rather extended line of customers on those old ring boxes that made up one of the last party line systems in Texas. I knew when the phone rang that it must be important. I also knew it would not be private.

It was Wallace. He asked me to "come on over" to the house of our three prospects. They weren't prospects any more.

Unable to sleep, this teacher had made his way to their home, got them out of bed, and helped them in their final steps to the cross of Calvary.

When he told me, everyone "else" on the line joined me in praising the good Lord for victory. It was indeed the stuff of which most church victories are made.

## Be Thou Faithful Unto The End

I once had the privilege of speaking at First Baptist Church of Monahans during the ministry of Bro. Levi Price.

I can still remember sitting at his study desk and noting a card inserted just under the glass surface of the desk, where he would see it every time he sat down to study.

On it was written a man's name and the day Bro. Price had visited him. Underneath that was the time of death of the man two days later and the heart rending statement, "If I had only known."

When I saw that card and the personal reminder to himself, my mind went back to an event at McDade five years earlier.

I went to my study at the church on Tuesday night to prepare for Wednesday night prayer service. But in spite of all that I could do, I could not "get going." My study went nowhere. My prayers went nowhere. I fidgeted and fumbled through about twenty minutes of this and then, finally I admitted to myself and the Lord that I knew what was the matter.

The night before we had attended an evangelism rally at Congress Avenue Baptist Church in Austin. D. H. Bonner had challenged each and every one of us to think of the most difficult prospect on our church field, and then led us to commit ourselves to witness to that very person within the next twenty-four hours.

My twenty-four hours were up, and I had not done what I had promised I would do.

But to be frank, I did not want to visit that prospect that night. In fact, I did not want to ever visit that prospect again.

I had been to that home on numerous occasions and been blessed out and ordered out more times than I cared to remember.

It was almost as though the Lord was saying to me, "If you are not going to keep your promise made last night, don't bother me about help for tomorrow night."

"All right," I said. "Let's get it over with. We can just go right over there to Mr. B's house and both of us can get insulted."

I walked, or strutted, the short distance to the impending explosion and knocked on the front screen, then stepped back fully prepared for a "bad experience."

The porch light came on, the door opened, and Mr. B. greeted me in a tone I had never heard before. "Come on in, Bro. Jerry," he said. "We've been waiting on you."

You can pretty well write the ending yourself. It was as though God had taken me at my word on Monday night, made preparation in the hearts of two lost souls, and then had to contend with the weak link in the chain — me.

The sad part of life is that the Lord seems much more willing to take us at our word than we are to trust in His Word to us.

# Although I Speak With The Tongues Of Men And Angels

The Holy Scriptures abound with examples of people who faced life with liabilities and found that God could turn those negative attributes into assets.

The hard part about learning from God's Word is the tricky business of applying the principles behind these examples to ourselves.

Toby Druin is the classic example of using the assets God has given us without being distracted by the liabilities with which we seem bound.

I shall never forget the summer Sunday at Pleasant Valley Baptist Church in Amarillo, when Toby and Laura made their way to the front of the church and shared with me the conviction that God was calling them to special service in His kingdom.

There was only one question mark which emerged during the conversation in front of the communion table. How could God use him to the fullest with what seemed a real and present liability?

He stuttered. Profoundly. He could hardly say two words without repeating the first syllable five or six times. All of the counseling, rehabilitation, coaching, or concentration had not overcome this obvious limitation to what most of us would accept as a "ministry."

But why did he need to conquer his stuttering in order for God to use him? What did he do for a living?

He was daily editor for the Amarillo newspaper, having come to that position from a similar position with the Borger News Herald.

The obvious question presented itself. Did he stutter when he typed?

No!

Instead of asking God to perform a miraculous act of healing to correct his stuttering, he accepted the profound truth that God had already performed a miracle by giving him a rare talent. He did not need to overcome his liabilities. He only needed to be a good steward of the assets with which he was blessed.

He went from that clear revelation to an act of commitment. He quit his promising job with the paper and moved to Wayland Baptist College, where he absorbed every ounce of journalism available. Then the couple moved to Waco and more journalism at Baylor University. From there he went to the staff of the Western Recorder and eventually on to the Home Mission Board's mission magazine.

The development of assets and the denial of the power of liabilities reached a fitting climax when he accepted a position of associate editor of the Baptist Standard of Texas.

Today, Toby Druin is Editor of the Baptist Standard, largest of all weekly denominational publications in the United States.

And he still stutters.

## Defining Moment

There are events, times, experiences in all of our lives which can best be described as defining moments.

Though we may not be aware of it at the time, defining moments shape and direct the flow of our lives to the extent that all of the events beyond that experience are set in time and place.

Spiritually, the experience of salvation is the ultimate

defining moment. Marriage defines much of our personal life. It is hard to find the experience that ranks any where near these, but I am positive that such a defining moment occurred in my life in 1963.

I had come to the end of my graduate work at the University of Texas. My allotted time before I started loosing hours was at hand. Dr. John Rath, my supervising professor was at the end of his tenure at the university and had accepted a position at Rice University. My dissertation was almost finished, with the accent on the word *almost*.

My dissertation was based on the evolution of Friedrich Schleiermacher as a German nationalist. The sources for most of the research were his sermons, lecture notes, correspondence, and his publications.

Most of the primary material with which I was working had been gathered and published in thirty one volumes after 1834. The problem was that the collection had been published in a short run of only four hundred sets, and most of these were in Germany. The ravages of war and the nature of time had made it virtually impossible to find a complete set with which I could complete my research.

No complete set meant no complete research, which meant no dissertation, which meant starting all over, which meant forget it.

After exhausting what seemed to be every avenue of hope, I finally decided that the best thing to do was to take a break from work and get out of Plainview. We decided to visit the Pannells, friends in West Memphis, Arkansas.

When we got there, Tab asked me to go with him while he attended classes at Southwestern College (now Rhodes College), a very fine Presbyterian school in Memphis. While he studied Spanish, I took my customary stroll to the library which was located in a beautiful Tudor style building over a hundred years old.

I walked to the card catalogue and pulled the "S" file on the chance-in-a-million possibility that they might have something useful on Schleiermacher. At that point I was approached by the associate librarian, literally a "little old lady in tennis shoes," who asked if I might need some assistance.

Then came the defining moment in my career. I almost said "no, thank you." She looked like she had been working in a dust bin, and it was hardly possible that this modest library could have what I was looking for, but I put on my most positive face and said, "Yes, I am looking for *Friedrich Schleiermachers Sämmtliche Werke*, all thirty-one volumes."

To which she responded, "Could you write that down for me?"

This was the general response to my inquiry at libraries when I mentioned Schleiermacher, and there seemed little reason to believe that much good was to come from it.

With my note in hand, the librarian disappeared down a stairway behind the accessions desk, and then reappeared and said to me, "Would you like to come with me, sir?"

Now turn the clock back one hundred years. A German Lutheran minister had landed in Memphis on his way to Nebraska when the American Civil War erupted. Stranded by the blockade of the Mississippi River, he stored several barrels of books at the library while he waited out the conflict.

When Nathan Bedford Forrest decided it was time to take his men east, some of the valuables of Southwestern College were placed behind a false wall in the basement of the library for safekeeping.

For reasons unknown, these barrels remained hidden for a hundred years until a plumbing problem and a water leak led to the discovery of the hidden treasure the day before I got there.

The assistant librarian had helped open one of those barrels and had picked up a book entitled *Friedrich Schleiermachers Sämmtliche Werke, Predigten, I*

At precisely that moment someone had asked for assistance in the library, and my new-found angel confronted

48

a frustrated researcher asking for what was now the most recent book she had handled.

When she took me to that barrel of books, it was like peering over into glory land. There were the perfectly preserved and nearly complete collected works of Schleiermacher. The folded pages had never been cut and the ink had never oxidized. All of the volumes I needed were there.

The rest, as they say, is history. Using microfilmed reproductions of the entire collection, I was able to finish my dissertation, complete my Ph.D., and had my dissertation published by the University of Texas Press; and followed a clear career path that led straight to my responsibility with the Baptist General Convention of Texas.

Ask me sometime if I believe in miracles.

# The Call

The assurance that we have been "called" of the Lord to any or all aspects of our careers, personal lives, and places of service is an elusive element in our day-to-day experiences.

I knew from the first semester I enrolled at Wayland that my call was to Christian Education.

Three professors, Ed MacMillan, H. Preston James, and Orville Yeager, counseled me to consider what they felt was my natural place of service in the Kingdom. Other tugs at my heart led me to make this my career goal by the end of my first year in school.

My exposure to the history of ideas at Wayland led me to transfer to Mississippi College for my junior year, so that I could complete a major in philosophy while I also majored in history and English.

Upon graduation from Mississippi College I was accepted in doctoral programs at three universities, and elected to accept a teaching fellowship from the Department of Philosophy at the University of Texas beginning in the fall of 1956.

Even when called as pastor at First Baptist Church of McDade, I told the church leaders that I felt that my primary call was to prepare for Christian Education, and that upon completion of my doctorate I intended to pursue that calling at a Baptist school.

An act of "fine tuning" occurred in my first year at the University of Texas when, with the concurrence of the two departments involved, I changed my program from philosophy to intellectual history.

In April of 1960, the time of preparation was at an end. My supervisory committee at the University expressed to me the conviction that I had completed the necessary residence for the doctorate. Time had come for me to prepare for the qualifying exams and write my dissertation.

Dr. John Rath , my supervisor, and Dr. Joe B. Franz, Chair, expressed every confidence that I should consider placement at a nearby state university so that I could conveniently pursue the rest of the doctoral program.

I thanked him for his concern, but declared my intention to locate with a Baptist college if at all possible. I realized that this was not what they wanted to hear, but it was what my heart was telling me. I left their office at 9:00 A.M. on a lovely Friday morning and made my way to McDade and prayer time.

Margie and I knelt in the living room of the parsonage an hour later, and shared our conviction with the Father that we had followed by faith to this point, but now needed His direction to finish the eight year pilgrimage of faith we had made.

On Monday, I received a letter from Dr. A. Hope Owen, President of Wayland Baptist College, In his wonderful fatherly fashion he shared with me the details of a meeting in his office on Friday morning.

Al Cornebise, one of my former classmates at Wayland, eight years earlier, and Assistant Professor of History at Wayland, had resigned from the History Department to complete his doctorate at the University of North Carolina.

50

Would I consider an invitation to accept an appointment to that position for the fall term?

The post mark was what got my attention. It was stamped 10:00 A.M. on Friday.

I am sure that God's timetables include plans made before the start of time. It just takes a little time for the letters to be processed. If you wait for the special delivery letters before you start your journey, you may never take the first step.

# Cowboy Preacher

One of the interesting benefits of service in a Baptist college or university is the opportunity of working with students who are preparing for the ministry.

Some are very forgettable, many are exceptional, all are willing to assist in every decision-making process of the institution.

Of the more than two thousand ministerial students (preacher boys) I have known since I started college as one myself in 1952, one stands out in a unique class of his very own.

The first time I saw Dick was when he arrived on the Wayland campus to enroll as a ministerial student. He had attended the cowboy camp meeting services of the late B. B. Crim over around Matador, and got saved. Two days into the meeting he felt the call to preach, and the pastor brought him to Wayland in time to enroll for the fall term.

If you saw the old cigarette commercials of the early sixties featuring the cowboys, then you saw Dick. That line of commercials depicted him completely, from the magnificent handlebar mustache to the broad shoulders and the clear eyes.

Dick and his wife lived in a line shack on a ranch and they brought their ranching lifestyle with them, which made them singularly unique among their ministerial peers.

51

And there was one other interesting side to Dick. He cussed. He was pretty good at it. In fact, he was perfect at it.

Dick could describe in detail, in appropriate Sunday English, a slow moving cow crossing the road. But if the cow started running, Dick started cussing.

Needless to say, he was a novelty. Many a church was interested in hearing the converted cowboy preach — once. After he preached on Sunday, the college switchboard would light up on Monday with callers asking, "Do you know what he said yesterday?"

Try as he would, and with lots of help from "proper" preacher boys, Dick found his cowboy vocabulary an almost impossible barrier to overcome.

After a while it seemed that there was more to it than a matter of words and vocabulary. It was not what he said that bothered some of his peers. It was his tenacious hold on his own identity. He wanted folks to accept him and they wanted to change him.

By the time he approached graduation, many of the wiser heads advised Dick that he really ought not consider seminary (folks there had never even heard some of his better expressions) if he could not leave his cowboy ways behind.

Thank goodness he took their advice. The kingdom was richer as a result of it.

The Home Mission Board and other interested parties saw in him a rare personality with a vast potential in a very special setting.

They equipped his family with ranch transportation and the tools of the trade.

He ended up in eastern Colorado as a missionary to the cowboys on the vast eastern slope. He moved from ranch to ranch, cowboy to cowboy, sharing his faith and his witness, and offering the hope of Christ to each and every one of them.

And one by one, cowboy after cowboy came to know the Lord.

Somehow, if he cussed, they did not seem to notice it.

A whole string of churches in eastern Colorado can trace their historical origin to Dick's cowboy ministry.

The last time I saw Dick, he was pastor of a Spanish mission in Silverton, Texas and was the duly elected county sheriff.

I have always figured that when he preached in Spanish, he could speak as fast as he wanted to without having to worry too much about cussing.

I learned from Dick a genuine appreciation for the concept of a "God-called ministry."

## Geography

Almost every college curriculum lists a number of courses which have made their way into the catalog and proven an adventure for everyone concerned.

At Wayland Baptist University that course was Survey of Geography.

The formal justification for the course was that it met certification requirements for elementary education.

The unprinted needs were as varied as the types of students who enrolled in it. Athletes needed three "sure" hours to stay eligible. Ministerial students had to have something to balance off second year New Testament Greek. Folks needed something to keep their adult education plans on focus. Some students simply needed something to hold on to as a point to their college pursuits, and had not found it yet.

I inherited Geography as my "fifth" preparation my first semester as a college professor in 1960. My background consisted of three hours of Survey of Geography, which I had taken in 1953 as a second year student at Wayland.

The fun began shortly thereafter.

Task number one, after only two days advance notice that I would teach the course, was to go to the bookstore and pick up the text for the course.

I was fortunate enough to finish all of my course requirements for the doctorate at the University of Texas by

the time I was twenty six. Aside from the haggard look that came from three youngsters and the pending dissertation, I still had the look of a student.

As I stood in the bookstore stacks looking at Freeman and Raup's survey textbook, an older man asked me if I were planning to be in that class. When I answered in the affirmative, he seemed to be relieved that there would be at least one more poor soul taking the course.

"I sure hope the bird teaching that course knows what he is talking about," he pleadingly suggested.

"So do I," I responded.

One of life's priceless doubletakes occurred two days later when I walked into the class, placed my text and roll cards on the podium, turned to my older, and now wiser, classmate, made two wings out of arms, and proceeded to fly.

Come to think of it, that was the only soaring we did the whole semester.

As one might expect, the whole class laughed and it served to take the edge off of a typical first day of class. But there was one exception to the response of the class. A young lady behind the older student seemed withdrawn and frightened and confused by the levity of the moment.

As the days passed it became all the more evident that insecurity was the word that described Jeannie's life. She was attractive but unaware of it, she was sharp but afraid to display it, wanting friends but afraid to make the first move for fear of rejection.

Halfway through the term I learned that she was a product of Buckner Children's Home. All of the behavior patterns then began to take shape and I began to grow in my admiration for a young lady who really was walking a tenuous path through life "on her own" for the first time.

Shortly after that, I was speaking at First Baptist Church in Borger, and alluded anonymously to Jeannie and her circumstances as a classic example of a person with absolutely no one to evidence concern for her well-being.

Following the service I was approached by a Mr. T.

who asked if it would be possible for him to come to Wayland the following Monday.

The next morning, during the most exciting part of my lecture on the influence of lateral moraines on the topographical structure of western New Mexico, a request come from the office of President A. Hope Owen to bring Jeannie to his office.

I knew the nature of the summons, but Jeannie did not. I actually thought that she would faint before we made it to the office. It terrified her to think that she might have broken some rule that might lead to her expulsion from school. Her hold on a secure place in the world was fearfully tenuous.

Mr. T. was waiting in President Owen's office. What followed was the most tender moment I have been privileged to witness.

He explained to her that he had retired that year from Phillips Petroleum Company. He was basically alone in the world and understood what it was like to know that no one was overly concerned about his welfare.

Then he said that he understood that Jeannie seemed to be in about the same circumstance.

He then presented Dr. Owen with enough stock certificates to cover the cost of Jeannie's expenses at Wayland. That was a very special moment.

But he was not yet finished. He then wrote her a very sizable personal check. He told her that she was to go on a spending spree. He wanted her to buy herself a beautiful dress, with shoes, a hat, and gloves to match.

"Jeannie, I want you to do this for one reason. Every time you wear this outfit I want you to remember that there is someone in this world who cares how you look."

Didn't Jesus say something about the assurance we have, that if God adorns the lilies of the field, he will surely care for our needs, too?

For some reason or another, I still remember that class with very strong emotions.

# A Load of That Green Stuff

Communication is an art form. When it comes to communications with regard to money, it is most often a lost art form.

I learned this lesson the hard way with Bro. Lynn.

Lynn was probably the most successful farmer I have ever known. He farmed dryland cotton and maize north of Tahoka, Texas, and made a bale an acre when everyone else plowed everything under.

He was also one of the most compassionate men I have known. I first met him while speaking for Texas Alcohol Narcotics Education, Inc. at First Baptist Church in Tahoka.

Lynn made a generous gift to this cause and was already known as a steadfast supporter for worthy community and county causes.

He was also a prime subject for development officers due to the fact that he had no immediate family, no will, and enormous tax liabilities for his estate at death.

Over a period of many months I tried to interest Lynn in the needs of ministerial students at Wayland Baptist College where I taught on the faculty of the History Department.

One morning, out of the clear blue sky, I got a telephone call from Lynn in Tahoka.

"Doctor," he asked, "are you still needing help for those preacher boys at your school?"

"Yes, sir." I responded, trying my best to suppress my excitement. "These young fellows need all the help they can get."

"Well, I have decided to come up there and lay a load of green stuff on the school," he said.

Mercy, me! My heart nearly stopped beating.

Then he quickly added, "Do you think you could take my picture?"

Silly fellow. I would get Cecil B. DeMills there if need be.

"You bet!" I promised.

56

"And do you think Dr. McClung would mind being in the picture with me?" he queried.

I assured him that Dr. McClung (President of Wayland Baptist College) would be delighted to have his picture taken with him.

"Okay," he said, "I'll meet you in the parking lot behind Gates Hall in about an hour."

Somehow it never registered on me that the parking lot was an odd place for us to meet. I spent the next hour rounding up the necessary ingredients for the appropriate level of honor to be bestowed upon a wealthy benefactor who had just unloaded his wealth upon the school.

Imagine the look on my face, and the faces of Dr. Mc-Clung and the school photographer, when Lynn drove up in a truck loaded with two tons of TURNIPS AND GREENS.

He had said quiet plainly that he was going to drop a load of green stuff on the school. My head had simply not processed what my ears had heard.

Do you have any idea how far two tons of turnips and greens will go on a college campus? That is enough to last till Jesus comes back, no matter how long it takes.

Knowing what to do with those turnips was one thing. Being able to express genuine gratitude was another.

Pictures were taken. Hands were shaken. An appropriate story appeared in the papers.

As a measure of success of all this, Bro. Lynn brought another load of turnips two weeks later.

As well as I remember, that was his last trip to Plainview.

A lesson about human nature emerged that should never be ignored. We usually do not make gifts to meet the needs of others. Our gifts usually originate and conclude with actions which meet our needs.

# Preaching to Ourselves

One of the first by-products of my teaching career was a sense of guilt over the surge of calamities which occurred whenever I elected to give a major quiz.

Strange diseases erupted, thrived, and disappeared without so much as a single medical verification. Toilets ceased to function. Automobiles malfunctioned. Very distant relatives seemed to die in clusters and always at least two states away.

I came to feel a terrible sense of responsibility for the obvious cause-and-effect relationships between my testing cycles and the mean old devil stalking the land to devour my students.

I also discovered that it was hard to be fair in grading a make-up quiz which had been brought on by my extra-terrestrial influence which was beyond the control of the student taking the quiz.

My first impression was to remove the cause for all of the discomfort by doing away with all major quizzes and drawing grades from a hat. Somehow, that seemed inappropriate.

By the second year of the test/feel guilty/give a make-up/feel guilty cycle I decided upon a new testing principle.

In advanced classes I would allow the class to vote on the day for major exams with the understanding that I would not give makeups for any reason. At the end of the semester I would throw out the worst grade of the semester on the principle that anyone could have a bad day.

The immediate results were remarkable. Viruses died aborning. Storms veered off at the last minute. Households became models of functionality. Cousins got well instead of going on to Glory.

I must add that my concept of fairness did not stand the rigorous test of time, but it led to the most creative intervention by the Holy Spirit in the life of any student I knew at Wayland Baptist College.

One of my ministerial students in the advanced Ancient History course missed a quiz on Monday. It was strange that he should miss the class because he was the one who led the class to vote for that particular time for the quiz.

The class met at 11:00 A.M., and at 4:00 P.M. I met the vanishing American halfway between Gates Hall and Van Howling Library.

His first words were, "I guess I am in trouble, right?"

When I tried to assure him that the end was not yet, he hastened to explain the reason for his fall from grace so early in the term.

It seems that he had celebrated his anniversary at his rural church near Lubbock on Sunday and the church had honored their pastor by giving him a Wollansach Tape Recorder, at that time the most coveted item among college "preacher boys."

He then explained that he had taped his Sunday morning sermon on his new preaching aid. The challenge of the recorded word evidently lifted him to new heights of pulpit artistry.

The test of the effect of his new preaching aid came the next morning . While he prepared to make his pilgrimage to Wayland for his quiz in Ancient History, he replayed his sermon from the day before.

To use his words, "Doc, so help me, I preached myself under conviction. I just couldn't leave."

What could I say? It was the Holy Spirit that had actually missed the test.

It was also one of the first confessions I ever heard where a preacher declared that he had been effected by his own sermon.

Come to think of it, it was the only time.

# Aggies

In 1968, after eight good years at Wayland our lives took an unexpected turn. Margie contracted pneumonia

59

and then had a violent reaction to her medications with a resulting hospital stay of almost a month.

Her medical team urged us to move as far as possible from dust and low humidity and do it as soon as possible.

Without a long series of details, I was extended an opportunity to join the graduate history faculty at Texas A&M University and help build the base for a doctoral program in European History.

I never really understood at the time why the Lord had led me to that place in my career, for I had made a very early commitment to serve the cause of Christian Education. It took eight years for it all to make sense with my nomination as president of East Texas Baptist College.

While all of this was unfolding, I enjoyed three wonderful years with some of the finest folks in the whole world. The only glitch was the realization that for a good portion of my life I had told Aggie jokes, "and now I are one."

I soon realized that, all kidding aside, Aggies really did not understand Aggie jokes.

True story!!! (Not that I have to classify my stories as true or false.)

On the very first day of class in September of 1968, I was about to enter my 8:00 A.M. MWF class when I was approached by a senior cadet (boots, clean cut hair, pressed uniform, the works), who asked me, "Are you the professor in this class?"

I responded affirmatively, and he answered with another question.

"Do you know what wears a white cape and rides a pig?"

I chuckled a bit at the question and assured him that I did not.

He chuckled in return and blurted out, "Lawrence of A&M!" Then he turned and walked away.

*Lawrence of Arabia* was the big attraction at the Varsity Theater and as soon as I tried to conjure up a picture of an Aggie riding across the sand dunes on a big boar with a white cape fluttering in the wind, I could not help laughing.

60

In fact, I could not stop laughing. It was not one of those "laugh and get it over with" types of merriment. This was way down deep inside. And the closer I got to the classroom door in Nagle Hall, the deeper and harder the urge grew to bend over double.

It was when I stood before the class that they noticed that something had really touched my funny bone. It was also then that I realized that there was no way in the world that I could repeat the Lawrence of A&M question to them. And that all served to make the urge to laugh irrepressible.

"What's so funny?" several asked.

"I can't tell you," I managed to say as I struggled to override the urge to laugh.

All that did was set off a chorus of "Whoops, whoops," in the finest tradition of Aggieland, coupled with a demand that I tell them my secret.

"Okay, " I said. "What wears a white cape and rides a pig?"

Well, they allowed as how they didn't know, and I proposed the answer, "Lawrence of A&M."

Immediately, in chorus, in unison, and in earnest, they said, "WHO'S LAWRENCE?"

So much for Aggie jokes.

I soon came to realize that the faculty were in the same boat as the students.

One day several of us had lunch at a new smokehouse across the street from the main entrance to the campus. As we left by way of the foyer, we passed an antique cream separator.

Here we were teaching in the ultimate repository of any and all information related to agriculture in Texas, America, the world, and maybe the universe. Imagine my surprise when one of the professors asked a general question directed toward anyone who could answer it.

"What is that?"

I figured that he was kidding, but he was not.

I explained to him in minute detail that it was used to separate cream from raw milk.

Milk was poured into the large open vat at the top and

the crank was turned until a rhythm was established by the sound of bells. When just the right speed was maintained, cream came out of one spout and was caught by a bucket hanging from a spigot and raw milk came out the other spout. The cream was placed in large cream cans to be sold to the creamery and the "blue john" was fed to the hogs.

A look of sheer wonderment came over his face, and then came the question, "HOW DOES IT KNOW?"

## Good Sportsmanship

Intense rivalries were the hallmark of the old Southwest Conference, and none seemed to match the intensity of the Baylor-A&M competition in 1969–70–71.

One game in particular had a dramatic effect upon my life and my career as a supply preacher.

The final game of the season found the two schools in a peculiar position — the winner of the game would be the champion of the Southwest Conference.

I do not remember many times in the history of the conference when being the winner of the conference trophy had much of an effect of substance on the course of human history. Still, it seemed important.

Forget the fact that it was just a game. Forget the fact that it was just a Southwest Conference game. Forget that it was a championship game. Take note only that it was a game between Baylor and A&M.

In dramatic fashion, everything came down to a final possession, a stolen ball, a desperate dribble, a crushing foul, and a riot.

An unscheduled prayer meeting occurred behind the Baylor goal, and old Ags felt compelled to help the Baylor folks get on their knees so as to be able to pray properly.

Crisis management meetings followed in College Station, Waco, Austin, and, probably, in North Zulch. Threats of legislative intervention, withholding of funds, marches,

. . . all of the gritty things of which true higher education is made, filled the media by Sunday morning.

Now enter Jerry Dawson.

Weeks before the big Saturday night event, I had been invited to supply the pulpit at Columbus Avenue Baptist Church in Waco. Oblivious to most of what had happened the night before, I proceed to Waco from Bryan, where I present myself to the Associate Pastor just in time to file into the sanctuary for the service.

Columbus Avenue Baptist Church was one of THEE Baptist churches in Waco, and heavily populated by folks who had seen, and PARTICIPATED IN, the prayer meetings the night before.

The nature of my problem did not become obvious until I was introduced as a history professor from Texas A&M.

That was all the introduction I got. It was more than I needed. I had grown up on the high plains of the Panhandle and thought I had seen severe changes in weather that were called "blue northers." The reaction of that congregation to my introduction made blue northers look pale green.

I had the distinct impression that they did not like me.

Twenty seconds is not much time to change game plans, but I knew we could not proceed with any type of spiritual worship until we had dealt with our more immediate problem of fellowship one with another.

I stepped to the pulpit, said that I was glad to be there, but that the Associate Pastor had made a mistake in introducing me.

"I do not teach history at Texas A&M." I explained with the biggest grin I could muster.

"I TEACH GOOD SPORTSMANSHIP."

It took a minute. Even Aggies would have gotten the point.

A chuckle or two was followed by a laugh or two, which was followed by a general snicker, which finally ended in a round of applause.

At last we could get on with the business that brought us together.

It would be nice if we could start every service with the same honesty.

## Custer Could Have Hired Us

My father's observation about "just being a person" served me well for almost thirty years. The day finally came when I had to abandon a borrowed idea of identity and test the idea of "discovering my own identity."

Was I ever in for a surprise.

The third step in my academic career began when I accepted the invitation of President Billy Mac Jones to become the Dean of the Graduate School of Southwest Texas State University in San Marcos, Texas.

It was a very difficult decision.

When I joined the graduate faculty at Texas A&M University in 1968 I had to get rid of about one-third of my best jokes. No matter. I had learned the first day on the campus that Aggies did not understand Aggie jokes. Because of the move to San Marcos, I was forced to slice off another third of the humor pie. It wasn't that they did not understand Lyndon Johnson jokes. They just did not want to hear them. (I eventually had to discard the last one-third when Baylor won those games that year.)

The first meeting of the Administrative Council of the University consisted of about twenty deans, vice presidents, and heads of various administrative units. Dr. Joe Wilson, Academic Vice President and one of the finest gentlemen I have ever known, opened the meeting by reading a letter from the education folks in Washington.

The letter was a long list of accusations, threats, and "final warnings" which were all due to the fact that Southwest Texas had failed to take the proper steps to employ a "native American" at the administrative level. The school was behind, an embarrassment, shameful, and perhaps

64

criminal. Somewhere in there was a thinly veiled threat to cut off federal funds unless something occurred, and that right soon.

Joe Wilson read the letter, shook a little, cleared his throat, and then announced boldly, "Folks, we have got to find us an Indian."

After a very, very brief moment of weighing the pros and cons of the decision I was about to make, I raised my hand and said, "Dean Wilson, I am native American."

Mercy, what a transformation! "How much?" he shot back. It must have been something like this when the gold strike was announced at Sutter's Mill. Somewhere in the back of my mind it struck me that if we had just waited, Custer would have hired us sooner or later.

"One quarter!"

"That's enough!!!" Eureka.

Off went a letter to Washington expressing gratitude for the leadership at the federal level to bring justice to the campus of Southwest Texas State. The Feds would be pleased to know that the newest administrator to be attracted to the school was a legal representative of the Choctaw nation. (It was amazing how good you could make an Indian look on paper.)

Back, in turn, came a letter praising the leadership of the school for "seeing the light." Where the institution had been behind, now it was ahead. Leadership by example was praised, etc., etc., etc.

Of course, all of this went to prove that my father had been absolutely right all along. I had been employed because of my credentials, not my lineage. They had not hired an Indian, they had hired me.

It kind of brought home to me the assertion by Paul that with God's grace there really was no Jew or Greek.

The tragic-comedy nature of the whole farce was brought home to me in about a month. Somehow, news had gotten around, as evidenced by a letter I received from a state university in California which stated, among other

65

things, that they had received a nasty letter and really needed an Indian.

## When Was I In Prison And You Visited Me?

While Dean of the Graduate School at Southwest Texas State University I had the privilege of representing that school in the Conference of the Borderlands.

This special international emphasis upon the mixed cultures of the borderlands between the USA and Mexico resulted in the signing of several agreements between our university and the National Autonomous University of Mexico.

During the rather lengthy process of negotiating an exchange program between the two institutions, I had the happy privilege of working with Prof. Anna Maria Maqueo, who did so many of the tedious translating chores inherent in such agreements.

When it came time to leave Mexico City for Texas, Anna Maria took me by the arm and literally begged me not to go until I had paid a visit with her to Santa Marta Prison.

Mexico has states much like the United States, and the City of Mexico is a federal district much like the District of Columbia, and has its own prisons for men and women. Santa Marta was for women.

It was through her insistence then that I came to know forty nine American girls who were imprisoned there. Anna Maria had developed an interest in them while teaching Spanish classes at the prison.

I was not prepared to see what amounted to a living hell. It is really not possible to describe the treatment of these girls, averaging in age about 21, at the hands of the guards and the other inmates.

Over half of the girls had never been formally charged with any crime, and probably half of those charged had never been tried.

Anna Maria confronted me with the awfulness of the moment when she said to me, "YOU, DR. DAWSON, MUST GET THESE GIRLS OUT OF HERE." It was not a request. It was a demand.

As she said, these girls were dying. She contended that no matter the charge or the crime, no human being deserved the treatment these American girls were receiving. But as she said, if I did not hurry, I might as well forget it, because there would not be much left to save.

Again at the airport she laid the charge to my heart. I MUST GET THESE GIRLS OUT OF THIS PRISON.

When I returned to San Marcos, what I came to call my Prison Project became an obsession to me. Of course, this same goal was being pursued by others, and much of what I did augmented what others were attempting.

What helped as much as anything was that Lyndon Johnson's presence was still a positive factor and the former president still called forth a lot of loyalties on the part of a lot of folks.

To make a long story short, I finally found myself on the phone talking with Señor Mario Ojeda, the chief legal authority in Mexico and somewhat akin to the Attorney General of the United States.

When I explained to him my concern for the girls in Santa Marta, he asked me pointedly about my personal interests in the matter. What was I getting out of all of this activity? It seems that a lot of folks expected, and received, considerable generosity on the part of folks for doing things like what I was asking.

I told him that my only interest in helping these girls was one of Christian compassion.

At this point he asked me the most piercing question of my entire life when he said, "What does Christian compassion have to do with anything important?"

I felt just like Paul must have felt when he testified before King Agrippa in the Book of Acts. The future of the evangelical missionary movement could depend on what Paul said that day. I instinctively knew that after all of the contacts, pleas, letters, and calls, the moment of truth had arrived. I knew that the lives of those girls could very easily hinge on the next thing I said

I told him that as far as I knew, Christian compassion was the only important reason for doing anything. Our conversation ended on that note.

It was my privilege a short time later to witness the arrival in San Antonio of a plane carrying forty eight American girls who had been part of a prisoner exchange with the government of Mexico. One young lady died before the exchange came to pass.

Perhaps with less evident drama, we daily bear the responsibility for the eternal future of countless persons around us. The very next thing we say can help shape the destiny of people we may never see again.

## He Is From Borger Too

Ask a public speaker about the best introduction he ever got, and he may have to ponder things a bit to remember the best. Ask the same person to recall the worst introduction, and the response is immediate.

Without a doubt the most memorable bad moment of introduction came from the lips of Dr. Paul Crall. It took a whole year, massive planning, and the perfect environment. It was the kind of dark moment that causes any public speaker to burn with envy that someday he might be able to do half as much to some other fellow speaker.

The first half of the introduction started with the ball in my court. I was serving as interim pastor for Castle Hills First Baptist Church and we were in that perilous time after the Wednesday night prayer service when announcements are called for.

Paul was the chair for the long range planning committee for the church, in addition to the less demanding task of supervising the physical plant for the University of Texas at San Antonio. He took his responsibility as chairperson VERY SERIOUSLY.

In his most professional engineering posture he announced that the committee would meet after the benediction in the general assembly area behind the auditorium, only to have someone break the solemn moment by informing him that the designated room was to be in use by another committee.

Not to be denied, Paul said they would simply adjust to the moment and meet in the parlor.

"Nope," said a voice from the dark recesses of the choir loft. "Can't do that. WMU got that all locked up for at least an hour."

Not to be denied, Paul pressed on. After two more peremptory thrusts, both parried, I felt compelled to observe aloud that one could only wonder about a long range planning committee that could not locate a meeting place in advance of their meeting.

With one single but notable exception, my one-liner seemed to arouse universal amusement. Somehow I got the feeling by the look in Paul's left eye that humor really needs to have a unanimous impact to be innocent.

Shortly after that I got an invitation from Dr. Paul Crall to speak the next year at the annual meeting of institutional plant managers meeting in San Antonio. It struck me as a little odd that a graduate dean at a regional state university would be called upon to speak to these "engineer types" but vanity provides a wealth of reassurance. Of course, I accepted.

Little did I realize that Paul did not plan a year ahead to listen to me speak. He planned a year ahead of time to INTRODUCE me. And when the moment arrived, the introduction consisted almost word-for-word of the following:

> Years ago my wife and I spent the night in a motel in Oklahoma. When we awoke, the room was filled with the worst odor we had ever smelled. I called the desk clerk and told him about this foul, foul, foul smell.
>
> He only laughed, saying that the foul odor in question was a chemical cloud that had drifted up from Borger, Texas. "It happens all the time," he said.

Then I stepped outside and immediately noticed a black cloud hanging over Goodwill. I turned to a man coming out of the motel and shared my concern with him about the possibility of impending doom.

He just smiled and said, "That's just carbon black. It blows up here from Borger."

About that time a rancher pulled up to the motel with a trailer full of Hereford cattle. The problem was that they were black and looked at the point of death.

"Mister," I said, "your cows look pretty sick. What's the matter?"

"Nuthin," he said. "They look that way cause I just brought 'em up from Borger."

Paul then paused for a moment of absolute satisfaction and said clearly and distinctly to his peers, "Our speaker tonight is Dr. Jerry Dawson and he is from Borger, too."

## Blend Into The Woodwork

Who among us has not at some time uttered the misplaced sinner's prayer, "Lord, please let me simply blend into the woodwork this one time and I will never get into this kind of a mess again."

I must confess that I have prayed that prayer more than once, which says a lot about the good Lord's powers of endurance, but I never was more sincere about it than the day in San Marcos at a reception given by Bill Crook.

San Marcos was a strange little Texas city, with several little clearly defined subgroups of strongly motivated political persuasions. The passions and politics of the late 1960s had pretty well shattered whatever semblance of unity there may once have been among the folks Texans loosely refer to as Democrats.

It was pretty obvious to the local political chiefs that some miraculous wand would have to be wafted over the city before the fall elections in order to prevent wholesale slaughter of the party faithfuls.

Enter at this point the Honorable Jake Pickle, congressman from Texas. Jake was one of those folks who merited the respect of the total community and who commanded a decent following whenever he came to town.

Since Southwest Texas State University was in Jake's "territory," I was not surprised to learn that he was paying an official visit to the campus. The story in the press was that he was simply there for a briefing on educational developments in Washington.

So, as the Germans say, "Die Stunde beginnt."

One of the deans walked up to me in the hall and said in a somewhat secretive tone, "Are you going to the Pickle reception?"

I had not heard of any formal meeting for Jake, but I knew instinctively that if a reception were held for him I certainly would be expected to attend.

My response? Of course I was going to be there.

He agreed to come and get me at my house at about 6:00 P.M.

Promptly at the appointed hour, Oscar arrives. When I started toward his car, he shook his head in bewilderment. "No need for that. Have you forgotten that it is just next door?"

I should have gotten a clue from that. Bill Crook was my next door neighbor. Bill had a long record of public service, including an appointment as ambassador to Australia, but he was not "tuned in" to university life at Southwest Texas.

As we walked the short distance to Bill Crook's back gate, Oscar gave me what I have come to call the "Best Man look." That is the look I see so often when the best man at a wedding looks one last time into the eyes of his friend before escorting him to the alter for a life-changing experience.

"Are you sure you are supposed to be here?" he asked.

It was at that moment that we got to the gate and saw Bill and Jake Pickle just inside. Invited or not, it was simply too late to turn back.

It wasn't until we shook hands and I stepped past the

two men that the dawn of awakening occurred. Around Bill's lovely pool were clustered three very distinct groups: one composed of a loosely knit coalition of university activists, local ethnic/minority leaders, and professional politicians; the second made up Hispanic leaders; the last, the clean-cut and neatly dressed WASPs from town.

You don't have to work your way through a McGuffey Reader to know that this is not a nice little handshaking reception for Jake Pickle, and that I definitely did not belong there.

It must have been the way Simon Peter felt when he caught all of those fish and then "saw it," knowing that he was in the wrong place at the wrong time for the wrong reasons.

I was not the only one experiencing the dawn of awakening.

Oscar looked down from his six foot six at my five foot ten through his very knowing bushy eyebrows and sensed a pre-suicidal panic.

His advice?

"Good buddy, you had better blend into the woodwork and get out of here as quickly as you can."

Good advice.

I waited until Jake climbed up on the diving board at the end of the pool and began his very relevant and soft spoken appeal for unity, and I breathed the misplaced sinner's prayer and beat a hasty retreat.

With the retreat came the hope that no one noticed my presence at the meeting. No calls came my way the rest of the evening, and no irate callers questioned my lineage, judgment, or sanity.

By the next morning I was convinced that I had managed somehow to avoid any identification with what could have been a very complicated and embarrassing situation.

Then I opened the newspaper. Yup. You guessed it. There, on the front page in a four column center fold was Jerry Dawson shaking hands with Jake Pickle at a local meeting of the big wigs of San Marcos political life.

It is one thing to get ourselves into situations in which we are embarrassed.

It is quite another to take the Lord along as an additional uninvited guest.

# General Flynn

Every time I see a movie about the Vietnam War, I get my own personal flashback.

The flashback I see is not related to the awful jungle scenes so many of us came to dread every evening on the news. Rather, it relates to the terrible atmosphere of hate, distrust, waste, and loss which found expression on so many of the college and university campuses across America.

In particular, my mind always goes back to the day in the early 1970's when I was introduced to an air force officer who had just returned to San Antonio from a bamboo cage which had been his home in Vietnam for six years.

As an American . . .

I saw a bright, handsome, decorated (but broken and used-up) man trying to put the pieces of his life back together. I saw a group of compassionate officers trying to get him the appropriate credentials so that he could become useful again under appointment at one of the military academies.

As a Christian . . .

I saw a man who desperately needed a door opened, a cup of water served, a visit to his prison.

As a graduate dean of a university . . .

I saw a monumental challenge to match his needs and circumstances with a specialized program that would enable him to return to the real world, in place of that awful personal hell he had endured.

Here was an exception that proved the rule. In record time, but with record participation by a great host of concerned academic supporters, he completed his degree and received his appointment.

Just another ordinary day in the academic life of a dean?

Perhaps. But about that time a question was raised with the state coordinating agency concerning the propriety and effectiveness of offering off-campus work under special circumstances at places like Lackland Air Force Base in San Antonio.

At this point enter another genuine American hero. General Flynn was to be honored with a parade in San Antonio and participate in a full review at Lackland.

General Flynn was reported to have spent the longest tenure in a POW camp of any officer in American history. He was honored and revered by the entire San Antonio community. And he was a friend to our newly graduated officer with whom he had shared confinement in Viet Nam.

When he contacted us to thank us for helping in the educational venture for his friend, he offered his services in the unlikely event an opportunity arose to express his deep sense of gratitude.

We shared with him the virtues of the program that had served his friend so well. Could he possibly find time to testify on behalf of this program? To this he gave an enthusiastic affirmation.

In between a magnificent parade in San Antonio and the military review at Lackland, General Flynn made his way to the Menger Hotel and gave his testimony.

All of this to say that there was electricity in the air as this genuine American hero took time from one of the finest days in his life to speak to the needs of military personnel he would never know but who might owe him their lives.

He said that he had learned to go through a routine which he followed religiously through the days, then weeks, then months, and finally years he spent in a bamboo cage which was being constantly moved to foil rescue attempts.

The sun would shine through the hole in the side of

74

the cage through which a pole was inserted so that his cage, could be carried from place to place. The spot of sunlight became his mobile point of reference.

He said that he created an imaginary string of American installations through which that spot of sunlight traveled until late morning. Then, in the afternoon, he followed the sport up the other side of the cage until sunset.

As the spotlight passed from imaginary base to imaginary base, he went through the military routine followed on each location. He issued and received orders, made command decisions, kept things in order.

He told that board of citizens that this technique was his sole hope of keeping his grip on his own sanity.

And how did he ever come up with such an ingenious plan around which to order his life and his claim to sanity?

He had taken a course several years before at an American military installation taught by a college with an off-campus program.

"I would sure hate to see this group make a decision that might someday withhold from a single American soldier his only hope for survival in his service to his country."

Needless to say, his position was honored by those present that day, and the opportunity continued for study at Lackland.

I have sometimes wondered if just maybe Jesus was doing something like that when he drew pictures in the sand when confronted by the accusers of the woman taken in the act of adultery.

## A Personal Moment With Lyndon Johnson

LBJ's love for Southwest Texas State brought him back to that institution on many, many occasions. He seemed to draw strength from the humble origins of his life, which he identified with San Marcos Teacher's College, as he often called it.

The last time I saw Lyndon Johnson was at one of

those special moments which all of us treasure. It was only a few weeks before his death.

The occasion was a special dinner to honor J. C. Kellum. Kellum had been a college classmate at San Marcos with Lyndon and had played on the varsity team. Through the years, Kellum and Lyndon had maintained a close business association, as well as a genuinely close personal relationship. Kellum managed much of the Texas communications "empire" owned by Johnson, and was probably as responsible as anyone for the strong financial portfolio of the Johnson family.

Only the love Lyndon had for Kellum could have lured him away from home on that night. When he emerged from the elevator on the top floor of the library building on the campus of Southwest Texas State University, he looked like a very, very sick man. His arm was in a sling and his hand was terribly swollen. It did not take an expert to recognize pain and fatigue associated with every move he made.

The announced purpose of the meeting was to inaugurate an athletic scholarship program in Kellum's name. Many of the friends of both Kellum and Johnson from the "old days" were there and the format was predictable.

I shall never forget the transformation I witnessed in Lyndon Johnson's physical condition as the night progressed. With each speech about the "tough years" and the "campaigns," with each reminiscence about deals and ideals, with each recounting of triumphs, Lyndon Johnson's body changed.

My wife Margie leaned over and whispered in amazement, "Look at the President." He was growing younger by the minute. By the time he was to speak, the swelling in his hand had literally vanished. The stoop in his shoulders was gone. The veil of pain and fatigue had been replaced by the look of the warrior on the eve of battle.

He was alive again. He was back in his "arena." He did not speak long, and I wish I could say that his words were memorable. The truth is, what we all saw completely overshadowed what he was saying.

As far as I know, this was one of the last public appearances for Lyndon Johnson. It was a very personal insight into the private world of a political campaigner.

# Is That You, Lady Bird?

When I went to work at Southwest Texas State University, the office I occupied was located on a beautiful corner of the library/administration building. My predecessor, Leland Derrick, dated back to Lyndon Johnson's student days on the campus. Dr. Derrick had played a significant role as a mentor and friend to Lyndon Johnson, and LBJ never seemed to forget this type of loyalty and support.

When I sat down at my desk, there were three telephones before me. Dr. Joe Wilson came in, and took it upon himself to explain the inner workings of the office. I asked about the reason for three phones, and he pounced upon the inquiry.

"That first one there," he said, "is the public telephone. If it rings, your secretary can get it. Of course, you can answer it yourself if you so desire."

What about the second phone? "That," he said, "is the inner office phone connected to President Billy Mac Jones's office on the second floor. You probably ought to answer that one yourself."

What about the gray phone with no buttons and with no dial face? "That," he explained, "is a direct line to the LBJ Ranch. Under no circumstances are you to pick up that receiver."

It was several years before the phone was disconnected, but I must make a confession.

Every day, without fail, I came into my office with an overpowering desire to pick up the receiver and ask whoever answered the ring on the other end of the line, "This is Jerry. How y'all doing, Lady Bird?"

I never did.

# The King Is Dead. Long Live The King

One of the lessons I learned in my very distant relationship with Lyndon Johnson was the fleeting nature of fame.

It was obviously an asset to work at a university where an alumnus was President of the United States. It was of considerably less merit once he became the former President of the U.S.

In 1972, three years after Johnson left office, I had occasion to call Washington, D.C., concerning a question involving Title IX.

In spite of my best efforts, I seemed to have a rather difficult time communicating with the functionary on the other end of the line. He was having a particularly difficult time determining where I worked.

When I said I was at Southwest Texas State University, he said, "Oh, yes. At Georgetown."

"No," I said very patiently. "That is Southwestern University. We are located in San Marcos."

Then I pulled out the old never-failing trump. "This is where Lyndon Johnson graduated," I said to him with all due pride and authority.

"Yes," he replied very dourly.

"That used to be important up here."

End of effort!!

Kiss Lyndon Johnson good-bye.

# A Seventy Mile Prayer Meeting

We often think of prayer as a vehicle for delivery of materials for miraculous construction projects by the Father. Sometimes prayer itself is an occasion for miraculous and wonderful things.

One thing is for sure. When you pray with folks, and the prayer becomes a special occasion for the celebration of

God's victorious handiwork, then the moment of prayer becomes fixed forever in your treasury of memories.

In February of 1976, I was caught up in work with a Kiwanis Club in San Marcos. We were seeking a special honor for our club within the Texas/Oklahoma District, and I was playing the part of the loyal civic club member in supporting the club's efforts.

This helps explain my lack of total surprise when I got a call at my office at Southwest Texas State University from Mr. Kiwanis himself, C. T. Bush of Athens, Texas. He was District Governor and one of the best known leaders in Kiwanis International.

He identified himself and told me that he and his wife, Rose, were in San Marcos and would like the opportunity to visit with me and my wife, Margie. When he suggested dinner that evening, my ego took a mighty leap forward.

Margie and I spent a most unusual and delightful evening with the Bushes. As one would expect, we immediately used Kiwanis work as a point of departure, but it was pretty obvious that Mr. Bush wanted to talk in much more detail about my administrative responsibilities as Dean of the Graduate School than my ambitions as a Kiwanian. It was also pretty apparent that Mr. Bush was very intent on delving into Margie's strong commitment to Womans Missionary Union work in our church.

Strange, indeed!

As we walked away from the restaurant to the car at the close of the evening, Margie looked into my heart with that knowing question mark she uses as a conversation piece and asked, "What in the world do you suppose that was all about?"

We both agreed that whatever Mr. Bush had been trying to learn from us, it most certainly had nothing to do with Kiwanis. We also agreed that there was something about the evening that extended far beyond a new acquaintanceship with two fine folks from Athens, Texas.

The next morning, Mr. Bush called me again at my office. He told me that he would like very much to meet with me again that morning, if only for a brief period of time. Always sensitive to what was appropriate, he suggested that we might visit in the office of Dr. Jack Byrom at San Marcos Baptist Academy.

It was at the Academy that I learned that C. T. Bush was chairman of the Presidential Search Committee for East Texas Baptist College. He shared with me the fact that he felt led to share our meeting with the rest of the search committee, and told me briefly the nature and needs of the office of president at the college.

I heard much of what C. T. said for the first few minutes, but I must confess that my mind started whirling so fast that the rest of the meeting was more like I was watching all of the conversations from a great distance.

Late in the morning I found myself back at my office, sitting at my desk and gazing out across the beautiful lake-filled campus of the university trying to find a few shreds of meaning in the previous two hours with Mr. Bush.

I was ignorant of any substantive facts about East Texas Baptist College. I had never seen the school. I had hoped for, and on occasion had even dreamed of, the day when I might lead a Baptist college, but the enormity of the moment simply overwhelmed me.

For the first time that I can remember, I was struck with an almost terrifying need to pray. I literally said aloud, "Oh Lord, I wish there were someone here to pray with me about this."

At that instant, Doug Hodo stuck his head into my office and said, "Dawson, do you need someone to pray with today?"

I had met Doug two years earlier when I served First Castle Hills Baptist Church in Castle Hills as interim pastor. He was the highly respected Dean of the School of Business at the University of Texas at San Antonio, and served his church as chair of the finance committee.

The morning of my visit with Mr. Bush was a troubling one for Doug. He awoke with an overpowering sense of urgency to come to see me in San Marcos. His spiritually sensitive wife, Sadie, finally urged him to take a day of vacation from the University of Texas at San Antonio and get on the way to see whatever it was God was doing that had created such a stir in her husband.

That was the background for a simple question, "Dawson, do you need someone to pray with today?"

I may not be able to remember today what we took to the throne of grace that day, but I can assure anyone and everyone that I shall never forget how God moved a university dean seventy miles to share prayer time with me.

Jesus said that the Father had not left him alone. He does not leave us alone, either. Sometimes he shows up wearing someone else's workclothes.

## Sick and Tired

My first day on the job as president of East Texas Baptist College was spent in Dallas, Texas, at the annual meeting of the Independent Colleges and Universities of Texas (better known as ICUT).

The meeting was convened at 9:00 A.M. by Dr. Maudy, provost from Texas Christian University, and an old-time veteran of the private sector of higher education.

Dr. Maudy began the meeting by saying that there was an awful lot of turnover in the office of president at private schools. In fact, he said, there is so much turnover that many of the twenty eight presidents at the meeting were new to him.

He suggested that a good way to start the meeting would be for everyone to introduce himself or herself and tell where he or she served as president, and also tell how long he or she had served in that position.

He then looked at me and said, "I don't think I know you. Why don't we just start with you?"

I proudly announced that I was Jerry F. Dawson, president of East Texas Baptist College in Marshall, Texas, and that I had served there as president for about ten minutes.

At that, the president of Trinity University in San Antonio leaned toward me and said, "I'll bet you're sick and tired of it already!"

# Meadows

The invitation to visit with the presidential search committee for East Texas Baptist College caught me long on interest and short on information.

It was the only Texas Baptist college campus I had never seen. And to the best of my knowledge, I did not have a single associate to whom I could turn for an in-depth evaluation of the institution.

Curiously enough, as I talked with a number of folks at the Baptist building in Dallas, the name Curtis Meadows began to emerge. It seems that almost everyone recommended him as a reliable witness to testify about the weaknesses and strengths of the Marshall college.

Having served there as a trustee for more than thirty years (thirty-seven by the time he went off the board for the last time), his name and the school were synonymous in the minds of many people.

When I called Curtis and explained the nature of my inquiry, I was overwhelmed by the response he gave me. His was the best single description of sacrificial service I have ever heard.

He said all of us make contributions to worthy and necessary causes and organizations in our community. Scouting, civic clubs, food drives, school programs—all of the special interests that keep our society alive and well. We contribute out of what we have "left over" or what they call in East Texas "front pocket" money.

He went on to say that many folks find special pleasure in a few of these civic and social services and end up on committees, boards, and drives. We end up supporting them. While we make contributions out of "front pocket money," we support with "back pocket" money.

In a few rare instances, if we are truly fortunate, we discover in all of the pulls and tugs at our time, talents, and money, a cause which is worthy of more than contributions or support. It is worthy of our sacrifice.

We contribute out of what we have left over. We support out of what we have. We sacrifice out of what we are.

"East Texas Baptist College is a noble institution." he said. "I have found her to be worthy of sacrifice."

He was right.

## Something Going Wrong

Murphy must have written his Law at a wedding.

There is no part of American society where perfection is more desired and less achieved than the experience at the altar. Practice, rehearsals, professional directors, mature couple, experienced ministers, small wedding parties, advanced reading — it makes no difference. Something always goes wrong at a wedding.

The beauty of it is that hardly anyone notices when some carefully orchestrated new idea is introduced into the ceremony and flops, or when someone says the wrong thing in the vows, or when the groom's shoes do not match.

That is what I tried to tell my son and bride-to-be as they planned their wedding at First Baptist Church. Again and again I cautioned them that they could surely count on the fact that things do not always turn out the way they are planned. They should not be surprised or troubled in the event that happened.

The very last thing I told them that Saturday before they went to the church to have pictures taken was, "Don't worry about something going wrong in the ceremony."

With that advice, I dressed in my tux for the evening and made a brief visit to a funeral home in East Marshall to pay respects to a noted member of our community who lay in state there.

At 6:10 P.M., two blocks east of First Baptist Church and

83

twenty minutes before the time when "something might go wrong," I suddenly realized that I had not checked the batteries in my camera.

"Aha, Murphy! You almost had me."

With that I turned smartly into a parking place in front of Matthison Drug. In my formal attire and optimistic best, feeling as good as I ever had in my life, I walked into the drug store.

And into an armed holdup.

This is known as SOMETHING GOING WRONG.

I really did not notice anything amiss until I got to the drug counter and saw the folks behind the counter "frozen" in their gaze toward two young folks standing in front of them.

I was in the middle of a sentence about all the trouble I had gone to in dressing for my visit to their store, when the young lady turned to me with what looked to be a .25 automatic Walters and requested silence.

For once in my life I was speechless.

Then she turned her attention to the druggist who was doing everything in his power to calm her by assurances that he would do whatever she asked.

All she wanted was Quaalude, lots of it.

The only thing I could think of was the story out of Shreveport the week before about a drugstore holdup on Saturday afternoon involving a young man and a young woman who took a large amount of Quaalude and then shot the clerks with a .25 automatic.

It did not help any when the tall young man with her leaned over her shoulder and assured us all, "She'll do it. She'll do it."

There was a very strange look in her eyes that seemed to back up his threats.

We are really talking about SOMETHING GOING WRONG.

In the brief span of ten minutes and a hundred feet, I had gone from lofty happiness and wonderful well-being to sheer terror and numbing inaction.

Then the druggist satisfied their demands, whereupon

the young lady left, leaving her partner in a state of confusion. He looked back toward the door, then to us, and finally asked, "Do you want me to go get her?"

The poor guy was in as bewildered a state as we were when he finally left the store.

While the druggist called the police, I looked at my watch. Ten minutes to make two blocks. A piece of cake. Police reports would have to wait until a wedding was over.

It was only then that I began to shake. By the time I got to the rear of the auditorium of the church, I was almost ill. Whatever juices there are that kick in during experiences like this had lined up and were marching post haste through my body.

Margie took one look at my pale face, sweaty skin, and blank stare and said, "I know you think something may go wrong tonight. See, everything is going to be all right."

Now it was back on the mountain top again.

Later, police arrested two young drug users who were convicted and incarcerated.

And Margie was correct. Everything turned out all right.

## Swing Low Sweet Chariot

Ben Rogers is one of those constantly striving East Texas Piney Woods evangelists who never became "empire builders" as is so often the case. Ben's greatest joy was his family of three gals and a fine young preacher boy.

I never ceased to marvel at his ability to put his entire family through East Texas Baptist College. When he was in the midst of helping his last two daughters complete their education, the whole process was wearing pretty heavily — as it would on any typical American family.

One day these Rogers girls came to my office with both hope and gloom. They had found a job both of them could do at the same time, and it would provide the means to help them through the rest of school.

Then the catch. They had to have a car. It did not have to be fancy — it just had to run. But they could not afford a car and had prayed for directions from above.

The Lord had convicted them of the propriety of sharing their need with me. In all my years in education, it was the only time anyone ever asked me to help them get a car from the Lord.

Within minutes after they left my office, a dear, sweet lady called from her home outside of Marshall. "Preacher" had died a short time before and his widow was clearing up his estate.

It seemed they had this "good old car." It was not worth much on the market, but it was safe, secure, and functionable. She asked if, by chance, I knew of a deserving student who could make use of the family car.

It was the only time in my ministry where a person wanted to give a student an automobile. It occurred within minutes of the only request for a car I ever heard.

Kind of makes one pay attention, doesn't it?

# Edwinna

The Romans surely had a saying (they had sayings for everything) that the greatest collegiate miracles occur the final day of registration.

As a college president I looked forward with eager anticipation to that last mad afternoon when the most incredible stories and the most incredulous requests surfaced for my benefit.

I somehow recognized the signs when Ed stuck his head into the office shortly after lunch.

Ed had been in my office before. Each time he barely escaped with his life. He came to school with a lot of bark on his trunk and it seemed my lot to knock some of it off each semester.

But this time it was different. Behind Ed was a tiny little gal with a pale face, a small suitcase, and a terrified look in her eye. He introduced Edwinna to me, explaining that they were childhood friends "back home." When he went home for Christmas, he had learned that her parents had each died suddenly and she was left alone.

He said that she had "no place, no folks, nothing." He could not go off and leave her by herself, so he had convinced her to come with him to college, assuring her that, "Dr. Dawson would know what to do with you."

With that, he assured her that everything was going to be all right, and dutifully "gave her" to me, and left.

She struck me rather like a fawn in the forest, ready to bolt and run, but with no place to turn and no one to help her.

I determined that we should do everything possible to get her into school. Now I learned that it was pretty difficult, even for the president of the college, to cut through all of the red tape, but by the end of the afternoon we had her admitted, registered, and housed.

The last thing I said to her after the ladies had pitched in to get linens for her was that I had done about all I could for the day. The rest would have to wait for another day — and by rest I meant the big question of finances. I hadn't the foggiest notion of sources of income from which she might draw to pay her expenses.

With that I left to go to Longview where I was teaching a January Bible Study from the Book of Ephesians at Forest Home Baptist Church. When I begin to analyze for the audience Paul's statements about being joint heirs with Jesus and part of a family of believers, I realized that I had witnessed precisely that spirit between Ed and his young friend from home. She was fortunate indeed to be part of an extended family.

As I pursued this line of thought I watched with interest the response on the part of a man who had come into the auditorium after we started the study. He was sitting near the back and had seemingly tried to strike up conversations with several people without having any luck. He seemed to hang on every word I said about the problems the youngsters had brought to my office and my attention.

At the end of the service, he made a straight line to me and told me an amazing story.

He had tried to find a short cut from I-20 to Hwy 31 and had gotten in the neighborhood where the church was located. Upon seeing the lights of the church, he had stopped to secure directions. No one would talk to him, so he simply sat down, whereupon he became interested in the story about the two college students in my story.

He confessed that he had not been active in church in years, and then confessed that he felt compelled to do something completely foreign to his nature. With that he took out a checkbook and signed a blank check. He told me that he would trust me with the task of filling in the amount when I had determined how much it would cost for Edwinna to attend the spring term. With that having been said, he turned and left.

The next morning I decided to make sure we all had the same amount of faith. I called his bank.

I just wanted to make sure everything was in order before I told the young lady of her good fortune.

His banker listened to my story, and then asked if the man wanted to buy the school. "He can, you know," he said. Then he said, "I do not know about that young lady, but he needs to give it far worse than she could possibly need to receive it."

The story has two endings, both good. She went to school, went home, got married. He went home, went to church, found a new meaning in life. I almost missed the meaning of the whole story. He did not help her . . . she helped him. And they both were better for it.

And I started looking forward to the last afternoon of registration.

# ✗ The Great Armadillo Raid

College presidents have a special talent for speaking clearly, distinctly, and understandably. At least, they all operate as if this were true.

About once a day, if they watch carefully, they discover that they are a significant portion of the population of miscommunicators.

A classic example of this occurred during the annual initiation rites for the freshman class at East Texas Baptist College.

The routines of initiation take on sort of a ritualistic nature with a climax befitting Barnum and Bailey. In the case of East Texas, the final night of initiation week was concluded with a march of the young ladies to the house of the president at about 2:00 A.M.

The scenario was always the same. They would cluster on the front lawn and sing at the top of their lungs. I would come storming out of the house and demand an explanation and an apology for the invasion of our privacy.

The gals in turn would offer to sing a perfect rendition of the school song (there has never been a perfect rendition of the East Texas school song.) I would make them sing it over and over until finally they would collapse and I would retreat into the house.

Then they would march back to the campus, passing near the boys' dorm, at which time the senior boys would lean out of the second-floor windows and dump pails of water on the poor bedraggled young ladies. With that, initiation time was over.

During one particular episode of this annual debacle, things changed. When I went out on the porch of the president's home, there stood the girls . . . with a new touch added. They were covered from head to foot with shaving cream.

In the hot, steamy East Texas August evening they were a most miserable sight with that shaving cream sliding off of them into neat little slick piles all over the yard. I

89

showed the appropriate anger at being awakened, they sang their song, and they were gone.

The next morning I made my way to the office while Margie went to the back porch to water her plants. There she discovered to her dismay that our back yard was a disaster zone, with huge chunks of turf uprooted from the yard.

Margie calls Buster Dysen, our supervisor of maintenance for the college. Every school has a Buster Dysen.

And with as much gentle compassion as possible, Buster explained to my wife that this was the work of armadillos. They were after grub worms in the roots of the grass. He assured her that nothing could be done about it except to plant new sod to repair the damage.

With that, Buster left and came directly to the administration building were he met me in the hall. The following conversation ensued:

*Buster:* "Mr. President, I understand you had some visitors at your house last night."

*Dawson:* "Yes, Buster, we did. You have never heard anything like the racket they made."

*Buster:* "Oh, you heard them? I have never heard of that. What kind of a sound did they make?"

*Dawson:* "Some folks might call it singing, but I can not. It was about the best they could do with all of that shaving cream on them!"

*Buster:* "Shaving cream??? I never heard of such a thing. Where in the world did they get shaving cream?"

*Dawson:* "Why, from those senior boys, of course. When a senior tells them to stand still so they can spray them with shaving cream, they really have no choice."

*Buster:* "I never heard the like in my life . . . and I sure do regret the holes they dug in your yard."

*Dawson:* "HOLES! WHAT HOLES? I HAVE NOT HEARD ANYTHING ABOUT THAT! How in the world did they make holes in the yard?"

*Buster:* "Well, Mr. President, they get down on all fours like this (personal illustration on hands and knees), and stick their nose down in the ground and just flip it over. That's how they made all of those holes in your yard."

*Dawson*: "Why on earth would any senior make a girl dig holes in my yard with their nose (absolute consternation)?"

*Buster*: "Girls? Who's talking about girls? I am talking about ARMADILLOS."

At that point a perfectly logical, but obviously flawed conversation came to an end. Old Buster and I laughed for days over this silly effort at serious communication.

Then I began to examine my prayer life and found that it is pretty easy to send and receive spiritual signals from God and come up with an identical process. Saying what you mean and meaning what you say may not always cover everything. Thank goodness God knows the difference between girls and armadillos.

## The Sky Is Falling, The Sky Is Falling

You are never going to believe what I am about to tell you.

You have never really studied the art of communication until you have lived surrounded by one thousand college students. You are often absolutely amazed at what you hear.

Texas experienced one of its most severe winters in the last hundred years in 1981-82. The bottom dropped out of the thermometers and stayed out for days.

Among the casualties from the prolonged deep freeze were the water pipes in several of the dorms of East Texas Baptist University. One building had frozen pipes for the first time in nearly fifty years, and one was a brand new men's dorm.

The terrible result was that many of the ceilings in the dorm rooms simply collapsed under the weight of the water and washed right out the doors like a river filled with debris.

All of this occurred during the Christmas holiday. Since most of the work crews needed to clean up the mess were made up of students, the only thing to do was send out calls for these folks to get back to the campus immediately.

In most cases, the students really did not know why they were returning. In one case in particular, a young man drove all of the way from Alabama and arrived about 2:00 A.M. His dorm room opened to the street much like a motel room, and he went directly to his room when he got to the campus.

The lights were off in the dorm rooms due to the flipping of the circuit breakers in the rooms. Not being able to turn on the lights, he simply got into bed and went to sleep.

The next morning myself and several other members of the administrative team were trying to figure out where to start in the clean-up operation when this young man came into Meadows Administrative Center.

In a classic statement of a student's ability to be totally unbothered by the real world, he said, "Dr. Dawson, you are never going to believe what I am about to tell you.

"When I went to bed last night, everything was just fine. But when I got up this morning, my ceiling was gone. I don't know what happened, BUT I DIDN'T DO IT."

Somehow I felt better after that about America's chances of surviving an atomic attack.

## Love God and Hate Borger

Let's face it. Being from Borger, Texas is not easy. It was one of the last of the oil "boomers" and was created ex nihilo (from nothing) in March and April of 1926.

It was so rough that in its early days folks said it was "Borger by day and Bugger by night."

There were even some who insisted that it was the only town in Texas where the whole town was on the wrong side of the tracks. And speaking of tracks, Borger may have been the only town in Texas which literally was at the end of the track. The rail line came "to" Borger but not "through" it.

I used to deliver the old *Amarillo Times* in the 1940s. My route ran right down Main Street from 3rd to 10th Street. I had a goodly portion of the bars and liquor stores among my meager list of customers, and I quickly learned to collect "every Friday" or kiss the payment good-bye.

How bad was it? In one summer stretch of three months I lost sixteen of my customers in shootings. Three of my customers were shot and killed on one day in slightly less than an hour.

To say that the population of Borger was unstable was to make the classic understatement of the age. No one was "from" Borger. There were no good old boys who had always decided things for the rest of the community. Everyone who came to the oil patch intended to leave as quickly as they could. The logical result of all of this was that folks did not do much in the way of permanent beautification or civic improvement.

Having been born in Borger only seven years after the town came into existence, my earliest memories of Borger are really the earliest days of the city. I still remember that there were no trees and no old people.

I also remember that there was a remarkable leveling of society in that oil field environment. No one cared where you came from, and in fact, never bothered to ask. Family lineage meant nothing. Criminal records meant nothing. Credit worthiness likewise meant nothing.

In reality, about the only thing folks cared about was your ability, skill, or willingness to work. No other real questions asked!!!

Come to think of it, that is not all that bad.

All of this to say that folks in neighboring communities had a rather jaundiced view of our fair city. The presence of six carbon black plants was enough to color anyone's view. The incredible odors which emanated from the oil refineries added to the image of the city as a bad neighbor.

And the bad news which poured out of Borger only reinforced the already tenuous claim it had as a civilized place.

The fact that it was one of the last Texas cities to be placed under marshal law seemed a logical result of its rough and tumble history. So what if the governor sent in troops and put the whole town under martial law for a little spell. Big deal.

The closest city with a claim to stability and permanence was Pampa. It had been a farming center long (as Panhandle folks count long) before Borger "boomed." One must remember that most of this part of Texas was only settled after the 1890s. There were not that many good old boys in Pampa who could count their stay in the area back more than one generation.

Pampa considered itself as good as it considered Borger bad. In reality it took comparison with Borger to make Pampa look like very much. The result was that Pampans regularly compared themselves with Borgans, and it always led to a very satisfying self-assurance that Borger really was "Borger by day and Bugger by night."

Maybe this will help one understand the second worse public introduction I have ever had as public speaker.

Bro. Claude Cone was president of the Alumni Association of Southwestern Baptist Theological Seminary in Fort Worth, Texas. His claim to eminence which led to this loft perch was the fact that he was one of the most successful and respected pastors among Texas Baptists, with much of this good reputation stemming from his pastorate at staid old First Baptist Church of Pampa, Texas.

It was customary to hold a dinner for seminary alumni in connection with the annual meeting of the Baptist General Convention of Texas, and the key ritual at the luncheon was the introduction of the presidents of the Texas Baptist colleges and universities, which furnished a steady supply of graduate students for the school.

No tribute was too stratified, no praise too lofty, no indebtedness too overstated. At least, this was true for seven university presidents as Moderator Claude Cone made his

way around the table of honor and lifted up the brethren
for applause and adulation.

When he came to me he said, "President Jerry Dawson
of East Texas Baptist College. He is from Borger. Well,
folks, on the wall of the nursery at First Baptist Church of
Pampa is a sign that says, 'LOVE GOD AND HATE BORG-
ER'."

End of introduction.

## Consider the Lilies

Jesus gave his followers a pretty lengthy list of personal ministries on which a good record was kept in our heavenly account book.

Visiting the lonely, feeding the hungry, giving water to
the thirsty, the list is pretty long.

Most fall under the category of "easily forgotten," and
Jesus was quick to point out that though we might not remember these acts of servanthood on judgment day, He
certainly would.

The most dramatic way for the typical servant to start
noticing the significance of kind acts in the name of Jesus
is to become the recipient of the acts of grace instead of the
giver.

This was my experience after back surgery in Tyler in
1981. I recovered on schedule from a triple fusion and returned to Marshall to get well and get going. Three weeks
later I developed multiple blood clots in my left leg and
went back into the hospital with a severe episode of
phlebitis.

I knew I was in real trouble when the doctor took my
wife outside the room to talk to her about my condition and
they both came back into the room with tears in their eyes.

When I told them that I wanted to know exactly where
I stood, the answer did not surprise me, but it did terrify
me. The doctor told me that I had very little chance of being alive the next day. If I lived, and if the swollen leg did
not respond immediately to drugs, I faced the strong like-

lihood of amputation. There was only one drug, a "new experimental drug called streptycianase" that they would like my permission to try, but they really had no way of predicting the results.

The doctor even suggested that, in the unlikely event I did not have a last will and testament, I should care for that immediately.

It was all brutally frank, but it was a direct response to my own request, and I needed to know it.

After signing a waiver, and after a time of prayer with my sweet wife Margie, and after a personal inventory of my life, I then found my self in the place of so many I had visited and prayed with over the years.

In came the nurses with this "last hope" miracle drug, and after a direct injection, an i.v. was started.

At this traumatic moment, an orderly brought into my room an arrangement of flowers. Ed Baker, a friend in Marshall, had learned that I had returned to the hospital, and he sent a sample of servanthood to help me.

The flowers were placed on a shelf. I could only see them by looking through the large i.v. bag of medications hanging over my bed. Suddenly I saw meaning in it.

Here was the best medical science had to offer me, and no one knew if it would be enough.

Through it was a picture of what Jesus said when he implored us to consider the lilies of the field. If the Father knew and cared for them, he surely knows and cares for us. With the best that medical science had to offer and the least that the Lord created, I was able to find peace, and turned it over to Him.

Needless to say, I kept the leg, plus multiple damaged valves, and I have kept to this day the image made possible by a friend who put me on the receiving end of an act of servanthood.

# Five Yard Line

The inauguration of Herb Reynolds as President of Baylor University was a splendid event.

The lineup of representatives from colleges, universities, learned societies, and academic organizations as is usually the case at such events was a most impressive sight. An added shine was given to the multi-colored hoods and robes by as magnificently a clear day.

By and large, most academic groups include a sizable number of, well, eccentric folk.

Caps and gowns are their only avenue to a look of normalcy. The unwritten but clearly understood rule is that the artificial appearance of order must be maintained at all cost.

The procession of delegates began in good order and moved past Pat Neff Hall toward Waco Hall, site of the inaugural program. Then, as is so often the case with such events, the procession stopped, and stopped, and stopped. There was murmuring in the ranks.

Representing East Texas Baptist University with her founding date of 1912 meant that I was fairly well back toward the end of the procession. It also meant that those of us at that point in the procession could see a very long line ahead of us and knew things were not moving. This gave a whole new meaning to "tenured faculty." Academe was in peril.

At that point a fellow stepped out of the line behind me. When word spread up and down the line that Grant Teaff was looking the situation over with a critical eye, there was a general feeling that things would start moving again any minute.

The robed delegate gave way to the head coach as he asked in his most authoritative tone of voice, "What's going on up there?"

To which a loyal but patient fan in the ranks replied, "We must have gotten to the five yard line. We have stopped there all year long!"

For a fleeting moment the staid mass teetered on the

97

very precipice of disorder. Decorum and dignity of the moment were lost.

## The Carey Workman Story

I have always been amazed at the seemingly random way in which God answers prayers. I received a call one day from a young pastor in deep South Texas. I had known him years before but had lost track of his ministry.

He told me that he pastored a small church and barely made enough to "get by." He had "picked up" a kid off the streets a couple of years earlier and had provided a home and love for a classic "cast-off" case.

He explained that his foster son had no resources and no academic talents to speak of, but he had a beautiful outlook on life and a great slider that always hit the outside corner of the plate. He had made all district twice on his 3A team and the pastor was certain that he would make any college team a "good hand." Would we help him come to East Texas Baptist College?

I got the particulars and alerted Coach Knipp. He began a heart-touching search for help and reported back to me one day as I approached the back door to the administration building.

He explained that he had been able to "package" assistance for the young player and had him almost covered. "Mr. President," he said, "I need five hundred dollars to wrap it up. Do you know where we can come up with that much for him?"

I confessed that I did not. At this point, Coach said, "Let's pray that the Lord will provide this for him." Coach was 6'7". When he said "Let's pray," we prayed.

I went up the steps, down my hall, and into my office. There in the office stood a young man named Carey Workman. The night before we had honored his daddy, Jewell Workman, for outstanding support he had given to the college.

Carey said to me, "Doc, I want you to know how much

98

we appreciated the honor you afforded my dad last night." He went on to explain that he, Carey, had been a ball player in college, and he was a pitcher. Carey added that he and his wife wanted to give the school a check in honor of his dad, but Carey got a rather apologetic look on his face when he explained:

"We want this to go to a young, needy baseball player, preferably a pitcher."

Whereupon he handed me a check for $500.

It struck me rather forcefully that this gave a whole new meaning to "going upstairs" to get a prayer answered.

# Ivey Miller

Prayers are like weather predictions. We do not always have absolute confidence that we are going to get immediate, particular, personal, undeniable, absolute answers to very complex and seemingly difficult prayer situations.

The most unforgettable answer to prayer I ever witnessed happened in Winnsboro, Texas at the home of Charlie Robinson.

I was a guest speaker for First Baptist Church for the morning worship, and during the Sunday School hour I was a guest of the senior adults. After sharing with the class some of the ways they could assist in the various mission programs of Texas Baptists, Charlie introduced himself to me and offered me an invitation to come by his home after the morning services.

He lived in a comfortable home on the north side of town. Charlie took me through the home and out back to a stairway leading up to a garage apartment which he used for an office.

Charlie was getting up in years and he was obviously very concerned about capital gains problems in connection with a very substantial stock portfolio he owned.

We talked for some time about various ways he could

avoid some of his tax problems by gifting some of his assets to tax free entities such as East Texas Baptist College (surely you would expect this to come up in our discussions) and by establishing charitable remainder unitrusts.

What really bothered me was the fact that we were looking at stocks which Charlie kept in his drawer, and the desk was only a few feet from an open flame space heater. I could easily visualize a disaster if this dear old gentleman happened to get inches too close to that heater.

I urged Charlie to do something pretty quickly, and told him all of the good reasons I could think of for haste, but I could tell that I was not making a lot of headway.

Finally, he shared with me his reservation about any type of personal commitment on his part.

"Do you know Bro. Ivey Miller?" he asked.

"I sure do, Bro. Charlie," I replied. I met Ivey Miller in the 1950s when he was associated with one of our Baptist institutions in San Antonio while I pastored First Baptist Church of McDade. He had gone on to serve as a missionary to South America and I had not seen him for twenty-five years.

"Well," said Charlie, "he used to be my pastor. He used to be able to give me the kind of advice I could understand about things like this. Before I could consider a gift commitment I would really feel better if I could just talk with Bro. Miller about this."

Visit over! Conversation closed! Where in the world would I ever find Ivey Miller, let alone get him to make some worthwhile suggestions to Bro. Charlie about that stock?

So, when there is nothing else that seems to work, pray. I suggested to Bro. Charlie that we should pray that the Father somehow find a solution to our needs by leading us to Ivey Miller. We prayed and arose and walked to the door.

When we stepped out on the landing and looked down the stairway, there at the landing stood Ivey Miller.

Mercy, what a moment.

100

He looked up at us, shading his eyes against the glare of the sun.

"Why, if it isn't Jerry Dawson. I have not seen you in nearly thirty years," he nearly yelled.

"Charlie," he said, "you ought to give him some of that stock you have for East Texas Baptist College."

Now, try that one on for a direct and specific answer to the prayer of a guy who was not even sure the object of his prayers was even alive on the face of the earth.

Oh, and by the way, Charlie did make a very nice gift to the college.

## James And Linda

Shortly after I came to East Texas Baptist College as president, a fellow appeared unannounced in my office doorway. He was on crutches and obviously in great discomfort.

He introduced himself and explained that he was a veteran and had just come from the Veterans Administration Hospital in Shreveport. His medical story was not good. James was suffering from a progressive disease of the spine. He would soon be unable to function on crutches and faced a future of bed-ridden treatment and a painful death.

James wanted me to go with him to the married students' housing so that he could break the bad news to his wife Linda. The experience at the home was sad. Jim cried, Linda cried, and I cried. It all seemed so tragic.

Shortly after that, Linda had to be rushed to the hospital to try and save her left eye. She had a detached retina and, unfortunately, nothing could be done to save it.

A few months later the same set of events reoccurred with her right eye, but this time approximately thirty per cent of her vision was preserved.

The doctor told her that she had better take a good look at the world while she could. She would sneeze, reach over to pick up something, or simply wake up one morning to find herself totally blind.

This time it was Linda who asked to have us go with her to tell Jim. "He's not well, you know," said Linda.

I must confess that this was an unbearable experience. A thirty-year-old man facing irreversible spinal disease and his 28-year-old bride facing blindness.

I did not pay as much attention to James and Linda as I should have in the weeks after that. One Wednesday a student told me that James and Linda were financially desperate and had nothing to eat. Their car was being repossessed and their utilities were being cut off.

A quick trip to their house verified the story. Sure enough, their cabinets were bare. They did not even have salt in their salt shaker. I called several folks to get food to them for that evening and then left for Longview, where I was serving as interim pastor.

The burden for these young folks was overwhelming. When I got to prayer service, I shared with the congregation the desperate plight I had just witnessed.

In spite of an understanding in that church about impromptu appeals for money, folks just got out their billfolds and purses and took up over $600 to help out.

I left the service to the care of the assistant pastor and hurried back to Marshall with the money. I must confess that I was worried lest James and Linda do something desperate as a result of what I saw as a hopeless estate. I could hardly wait to give them the money and also tell them that a banker was prepared to "take care" of the car note.

When I arrived at the humble home of James and Linda, the lights were out. When I got to the front door, I was surprised to hear the sound of two people, sitting in the darkness, singing a hymn of praise.

That was literally more than I could grasp. I asked James, "How can you sing at a time like this — with health and sight gone, no money, no food, nothing?"

Their answer?

James said, "What else can we do? God knows the situation we are in."

Linda graduated as a certified school teacher though legally blind. James saw the rate of deterioration decrease. They grew in the Lord.

No wonder John was instructed in the Revelation to remind the Church in Smyrna,

"I KNOW THY TRIBULATIONS"

## I Have Bread You Do Not Know About

The death of a loved one brings out a vast assortment of human responses.

Most of the things we try to do for others during the time of grieving falls far short of what we intend, but we generally have a feeling that folks understand what we are trying to convey, even when we do a poor job of it.

Two men came into my office at East Texas Baptist College on one of those missions of love and compassion. Their mother had passed away in Atlanta, Texas, and they as brothers had decided to establish a scholarship fund in her name. There was an obvious concern in everything they said, that their mother should be remembered well, and it seemed fitting to them, and to me, that what they proposed was an appropriate response to their mother's caring life.

Both brothers stressed the point that their mother was not a highly visible person and always chose to live out the role of a servant rather than a leader.

As the day wore on I became somewhat anxious about the funeral service the next day in Atlanta. I had an uneasy feeling that this dear lady might not have been too well known in the city, and that her life of servanthood might not be appropriately acknowledged.

I found my way to First Baptist Church in Atlanta the next morning well in advance of the time for the service. It was a good thing I got there early, as the church was filled.

Whatever fears I had that her death might pass unnoticed was immediately dispelled.

As I listened to people talk outside the building and in the vestibule, I got the distinct impression that many of the people who had come to the service had experienced the same anxiety I had felt.

I also got the clue to the reason so many of them felt compelled to show their respects.

Every person around me recalled a time of grief or sorrow or family crisis when this dear lady had appeared at their door with a loaf of fresh bread. In fact, the baking of bread in a time of need seemed to be the common denominator that tied together every person at the service.

The wonderful thing about it all was that almost everyone expressed surprise that this dear lady had done this for others, too. Her servanthood was universal, equal, compassionate, and very private.

I submit that when Jesus said He had bread that we did not know about, He might have named her as an exception to His rule.

# Music Man

I have grown increasingly amazed at the efficiency with which the Lord of Time and Space can coordinate the sending and equipping of the saints.

This was particularly evident one October evening when I traveled to Southside Baptist Church in Palestine for what was advertised as a Harvest Banquet. The church celebrated the year of mission accomplishments and focused on the needs yet unmet that needed attention from the congregation.

The service was in the educational building and the seating was by tables, and the arrangements did not lend themselves to an invitation. The pastor had indicated that I should feel free to make an evangelistic appeal if I felt led, and I almost did not.

I simply asked everyone to bow their heads and, if they felt led, they should make their way to me and share with me what was on their hearts. Therein was the story for the evening.

The first two who came forward were husband and wife. Carey stated that they had felt the call to commit their lives to full-time music ministry, but had never been able to get to the place where they could catch up with their bills, "cut loose," and go to school full-time. The best they could manage was part-time work at a nearby junior college. Now they were ready to test the Lord by committing themselves to go to East Texas Baptist College.

I could tell that this was not a problem I could solve for them standing in front of a congregation during an invitation. I was not certain that theirs was a problem I could solve in any event. The best I could do was to ask them to be seated and let me talk with them after the service.

At this point another husband/wife family stepped to me and made the most amazing disclosure. They had jointly arrived at the conclusion that they had been overly selfish in using the many resources God had entrusted to their care. They cited Christmas as an example. According to them, they had spent far too much on presents, and neglected to search for a mission cause in which they had an interest.

When I asked them if they had any mission cause in mind, they both agreed that they would love to help some fine young couple that might be interested in a ministry in music.

It is at that point that the hair stands up on the back of your neck. I suggested that at the end of the service I was prepared to join two families in holy matrimony.

As it turned out, the needs and the provisions were practically equal. Surprised?

Look at your own life carefully and you will recognize the same holy timing and the same adequate provisions.

# Joy

Watching people grapple with the complexities of saying "good-bye" is part of the experience of being a college administrator. By its very nature, the college is a place where students learn to begin novel and unique paths, and to severe old ties and traditions.

About the time I thought I had experienced the full range of farewells, I watched Joy and her Southern Baptist missionary parents go through the hard process of departing from U.S. soil and leaving her in school in Marshall.

They had come home for their furlough and had enrolled their daughter for her first college year, and now they were going back to the Orient and she would begin her sophomore year. Having never spent time apart, and knowing the full implications of their being half a world away, it was easy to see why they held on to one another as long as they could before they boarded their flight and she returned to school without them.

When I went to the office the next day to pick up my usual pile of letters and cards, I was struck by the fact that there were only two letters there. It was almost like a spotlight was focused so that I could not possibly miss the significance and importance of what I was to read.

The first was a hand-written note from Joy.

She recited with grace and gratitude that her parents, with the help of scholarships and the Margaret Fund, had made it possible for her to attend college. Her room, board, tuition, fees, and books were cared for. She also noted that the limited resources of the missionary family meant that they really did not know how her day-to-day living expenses would be met.

Joy then made the most mature and touching request I ever heard from a college student. She expressed the conviction that the Heavenly Father would not have brought her around the world and then separated her and her parents without making provision for her needs. Her prayer

106

was that WHEN GOD MOVED TO MEET HER NEEDS she wanted me to remind her to say THANK YOU.

Under Joy's letter was a letter from the Baptist Foundation of Texas. Lynn Craft and Tal Roberts expressed sincere pleasure in dealing with a unique problem for the Foundation.

Two decades earlier, George and Nettie Hughes had made arrangements with the Foundation to set aside assets which someday would mature. When the time of maturity for the trust occurred, income from that trust was to be used to assist children of missionaries under appointment by the Foreign Mission Board of the Southern Baptist Convention to attend East Texas Baptist College.

They cautioned me to take note of an interpretation of the trust which was unusual. These funds could not be used for expenses for tuition, fees, room, or board. These funds could only be used for daily living expenses.

Hallelujah!

Before Joy was born, the Heavenly Father had already touched the heart of two dear saints to reach forward in time to meet the specific needs of a faithful missionary family and a trusting daughter whose only request was to be reminded to say thank you when God did his wonderful work.

## Like Father, Like Son

In 1951 Wayland Baptist College took the unprecedented ethical high ground among Southern Baptist educational institutions when it opened its doors to black students.

The reason given was that it was "the right thing to do."

George May and Bonnell Williams were the first black students to graduate as a result of this courageous stand. In 1952 I enrolled in Wayland, and became the beneficiary of their friendship which I treasure to this day.

Bonnell had that wonderful sing-song manner of speaking so common among the folks from the Caribbean, and worked in the print shop with a special kind of life rhythm so common to folks who have walked with the Lord.

I lost contact with Bonnell after 1954. I had heard that he had returned to his native island home just off the coast of Columbia and that he was pastoring a native Baptist church there, but I knew little else about him.

Imagine my surprise when I got a call while at East Texas Baptist College in the late 1970s from Bonnell. It took only a little catching up for me to know that he was indeed pastoring a small Baptist church on an island off the cost of Columbia.

He told me that he had a son named Edison who "had light in him" and desperately needed to attend a Baptist college. After much prayer he had decided upon East Texas Baptist College.

Then came the question. Would we accept Edison? And more, would we be able to provide assistance?

As Bonnell carefully explained, if we accepted Edison, it would require a miracle to keep him in school. He had enough funds to get his son to Shreveport, but no more. There would not even be enough left over to get Edison back to Columbia if things did not work out.

When I asked him the basis for his conviction that we might launch out in a faith venture like this, he said that Bill Marshall had that kind of faith when Bonnell started to school at Wayland Baptist College. Surely the good Lord had not lost His touch in twenty-five years.

That was good enough for me. I told him to get Edison on the plane, and we would figure the rest out when he got to East Texas.

Not much of the unusual about this little episode thus far. Just another needy student with high hopes and low resources?

Wrong!!!

I got a call the next morning from Center, Texas, a fine little town due south of Marshall. B. D. H. told me that the men of First Baptist Church had had a breakfast that morning at the church, and the talk had centered around foreign students from our mission fields.

Bro. B. said that they had been moved by the fact that they had not taken on any special mission project in a long while. His question? "Would you folks happen to have a youngster from South America who might need a little help going to school?"

For some reason or other I tried to be very casual about what I knew to be a very direct answer to prayer. "Yes," I said.

"And where is he right now?" he asked.

"Somewhere between here and South America," I responded.

"And just how much help does he need?"

In my most casual of all casual manners I said, "ALL YOU'VE GOT!"

Three days later Edison was in the finishing process of registration at East Texas Baptist College. We had magically turned him into a painter (buildings, not portraits) only to learn that he painted in Spanish. We also found that he was quite bright and eligible for a special scholarship.

He had just come from Financial Aid and was carrying a piece of paper on which was written the seemingly fatal words, "Dr. Dawson, he still needs $500.00."

Edison met my secretary at the door to my office. She had just come from the mail room and had in her hand a letter from B. D. H. in Center, Texas. The envelope contained fourteen checks totaling exactly $500.00.

Bonnell had been absolutely correct. The Father had not lost His touch in twenty-five years.


## Foot in the Mouth Moose


Every development officer has a story to tell about the big one that got away.

There are not many pre-Civil War plantations still in-

tact in Texas, and very few are available to educational institutions for preservation and use in a restoration setting.

You can easily imagine the excitement I felt when an
heir to a beautiful plantation estate near Marshall called
my office for an appointment with the avowed purpose of
gifting the plantation to the college.

The owner had come to realize that inheritance laws
being what they were, when he inherited the plantation he
would probably have to dispose of the property simply to
meet the tax obligations incurred through inheritance.

The thought occurred to him that he could gift the
plantation to the school. This would get it out of the tax
stream. His dream was for the school to use the plantation
house and grounds as a conference center, and dedicate
the holdings as a natural preserve.

Needless to say, the idea of such an asset being transferred to the school with such enormous potential for historical and social benefits set my historical heart to pumping.

Dr. Gwin Morris, Vice President for Academic Affairs
at East Texas Baptist College, was also excited about the
prospects. He was chairman of the county historical society
and a key component in the network of Texas historians
who are dedicated to the preservation of historical sites.

Gwin and I sat down with the prospective donor and
began to dream the dream with him. The very first item
that seemed to require a little attention was the restoration
of the plantation house to its historical presence.

In a few words, it would be vital to put the manor back
to the time and ways of the 1850s. As soon as we brought this
up, it was obvious that we had hit a stump in the furrow.

Our donor did not immediately grasp the need to
make any changes whatsoever in his plantation manor
house. He liked it just the way it was.

We tried to reassure him that the need for restoration
was certainly no reflection upon his tastes in furnishings or
decor. It simply was necessary to give historical authenticity to the project.

When it was still obvious that we were not making any

headway, Gwin decided that a good illustration might make the proposal a little easier to understand.

"Authenticity is vital," he said. "Take for example our fine Harrison County Historical Museum here in Marshall. We have a classic example here of a very fine museum with authentic examples and memorabilia from almost every page out of our noble past for the last one hundred and fifty years."

"Yes," he responded with obvious enthusiasm, "it certainly is a fine museum."

"And when you go in through the main entrance," said Morris, "the first thing you see is a great big moose's head hanging on the wall. We all know that there never has been a moose in Harrison County. It is not authentic. It doesn't belong in there."

And then, to finally cap off his argument, Dr. Morris added, "And besides all that, it isn't even a very good moose's head. Big chunks of hair are constantly coming out of it and the poor thing is slightly cross-eyed."

Case closed, Prosecution rests. Hurrah for authenticity.

At which point our prospective donor stood, gathered his pictures and drawings into a neat pile and stored them in his briefcase, and then announced in his best Gettysburg Address format, "I'll have you know that I donated that moose head to that museum."

With that having been said, he left.

IT left with him.

## More Precious Than Silver and Gold

Don Anthony was one of the bright lights among Texas Baptist educators. He made the traditional pilgrimage of service from his graduation from East Texas Baptist College to the office of Director of the Christian Education Coordinating Board.

He discovered shortly after joining the Baptist General Convention of Texas that he had cancer, incurable, and then made another pilgrimage, not toward service, but toward death.

Almost exactly a month before his death, I saw Don in the reception area of the Bennett Student Center at East Texas Baptist College. Don was the president of the Alumni Association, and the executive committee of that group had their regularly scheduled meeting on this particular day.

I had not seen Don for some time and did not expect to see him at the meeting. One can easily picture the shock and surprise I registered when I saw him. He was brown, wasted away, and frail. Hardly a hundred pounds, Don was obviously in pain.

His story that day was a picture of the life he had lived.

Don had ridden to Marshall on a special mattress in the back of a van due to the physical discomfort he experienced in riding. I assured him that no one expected him to endure such pain for the sake of an alumni meeting. When I asked him why he felt compelled to attend this particular meeting, he gave the following testimony.

He told me that he actually enjoyed a luxury in knowing the approximate time and place of his death. He said that in the process of death he had been able to sort through the values of every element of his life.

He had worked for nearly ten years to finally arrive at his doctoral degree. Now, he noted, that degree was not exchangeable for anything of value in his life. In fact, he said, the only thing of value he still possessed that he had discretionary power over was time.

As Don said, he had about thirty precious days left on this earth. Time was the only thing of value he had left. He loved his alma mater, East Texas Baptist College, so much that he had decided to give her the most precious possession he had.

He would give his school a day of his life.

I saw the school receive millions of dollars in gifts during my stay as president. None matched the purity and grace of Don Anthony's gift of one day of his life.

What Don said about his gift is actually true for each of

112

us. The difference between Don and the rest of us is that he knew how many days there were left.

## Giving All That We Possess

Problems related to money, or the lack thereof, are generally the most readily solved. If you need ten dollars and you receive ten dollars, you have seemingly solved your problem. Finite problems have finite solutions.

Often money problems are really human relations problems wearing a very clever disguise.

Such was the case when the Director of Alumni Affairs came to my office and told me that one of our students was in his office in a deeply perplexed state. Her grandparent was dying in Arkansas and she desperately needed to go home but did not have the money.

I asked him to see what we could do to help.

By the time the young lady came to my office she had been steadied somewhat by the support others had given her. Word had gotten around and various people in the offices had taken up a little collection to help her.

The show of support was really more than she had anticipated. She explained to me that this was the last of her living, close relatives. Her grandmother was very important to her, and I could tell that it was extremely important to this young lady that she be able to be by her grandmother's bedside in what was obviously the last hours of her life.

The fact that others would go out of their way to help her was a source of comfort that obviously extended beyond the finite need of travel money.

She told me that her only way to get to her grandmother's house in Arkansas was to take the bus and she had almost enough to buy the round-trip ticket.

In fact, she said, she needed only one dollar to have enough to purchase her fare and be on her way to be with her grandmother.

Obviously, any one of us could have supplied that extra dollar, but just before she had stepped into the door to see me I had opened one of those letters that just captures your attention the moment you look at it.

The letter was addressed in pencil in very unsteady and wavering handwriting to the president of the College of Marshall.

East Texas Baptist College had not been known as the College of Marshall since 1942. So the handwriting and the address indicated that this letter had been written by a very elderly person.

The envelope was a kind that I had not seen in a long, long time. It showed all of the evidence of having been in a drawer or a purse or among personal belongings, and was crinkled and tattered. The glue had long since faded and a piece of tape took its place.

Inside was a brief note written on what seemed like a torn-out page from a Big Chief tablet. The handwriting was large and in pencil and obviously very infirm.

The author explained that she was trying to get things in order and she wanted to send the enclosed money to help some worthy young person at the College of Marshall. Enclosed was a dollar bill.

But it was not just an ordinary dollar bill. It was a dollar bill that had been rolled and unrolled and folded and held and touched until it had almost lost its identity as currency.

She simply signed the letter, Mrs. B———.

Here was a young lady who desperately needed one dollar and here was someone who obviously wanted to help a young person and had provided a dollar. So I gave it to the young lady and she went merrily on her way.

In a short while I turned my attention to the return address on the envelope. It seemed to me that surely there was a story behind this letter.

I was not able to pursue it immediately, but in a week or so Harvey Lewis, Vice President for Development, and I were in Shreveport and we located the rest home where this lady had been a resident.

114

They informed us that she had been buried a few days before.

They also told us that just a little while before she died she put her house in order. She used the last envelope, her last stamp and literally sent the last penny she had on this earth to the "College of Marshall" to help some needy young person.

To this day I have wished that she and the young lady could somehow have known one another.

It came very, very close to the Lord's description of the widow's mite. It was also the last and only time in my entire period of service in Baptist work where I saw someone literally give all they had.

# Lady on the Wall

On a trip to Europe in 1984, we ended up one beautiful morning in Lucerne, Switzerland. Margie had already determined that this was the day when she would put a big hole in me with the purchase of a "nice" watch.

"Nice" always is translated "expensive."

So, while she hit the watch stores on the lakefront, I used this as a perfectly reasonable time to visit the medieval wall which cuts across the peninsula on which the city of Lucerne was built. The theory being that this was the farthest point I could occupy from the watch counters.

So I and my credit card were walking together along the marvelous old wall with its seven perfectly restored towers and enjoying the fabulous view of the city, the lake, the mountains. The wall is built in such a way that once you get to the battlements you almost have to walk the entire length of the wall to get back down to ground level.

I was approached by a family unit — a grandmother type in her fifties (like me), a son /daughter-in-law type in their thirties, and a grandson type.

The grandmother walked up to me and in perfect and precise German said to me, "Excuse me, sir. Could you please tell us of a place where we can roost on this wall?"

I should have gotten a clue from her German. The Swiss speak an unusual German dialect, but I could understand her perfectly. But I instinctively knew that she did not want to roost on that medieval wall overlooking Lucerne.

I responded by saying, "I am so sorry. Your German is so good and mine is so bad, and I am sure I did not understand what you just said. Would you repeat it for me?"

"Oh, no." she said. "Your German is excellent. It is my dialect which is bad. But could you please tell us where we might squat on this wall?"

The first reference was to roosting like chickens on top of a hen house. The second was like a mother hen settling down on a nest of eggs or a pig squirming down into the mud. Somehow, I knew that we were missing something in our conversation.

For the second time I apologized and told her that I was sure that I had misunderstood her and asked again what she really wanted.

At the point, the son stepped forward and in his best Arkansas Ozark drawl told his mother, "Ast him if he can speak any English."

Yup. They were from Little Rock. They were tired and were looking for a park bench where they could sit down and rest a while.

After we all got through the laughter and the introductions we both saw some meaning to our experience.

She had looked in her dictionary and was working her way through words she thought might mean what she wanted. She was making her request in perfect expressions but it was not really what she wanted.

Our prayer life is a lot like that. Thank goodness the Father knows when we want to squat, when we want to roost, and when we want to sit, even if we do not know exactly how to ask for it. And he knows when not to answer a prayer in spite of the eloquence of our appeal.

# Waitress in Memmingen

In 1983, Margie and I went to Europe to plan a group tour for the next year. Since we were on our own and freelancing it, we were not in any particular group, but rather caught whatever bus American Express had available to get us to the next preview site.

We ended up in Munich one morning with plans to catch an American Express tour bus from there to Strasbourg, where we were to catch a Rhine cruiser.

The tour group we joined was made up of sociologists and psychologists from Georgia, who had attended a conference in Vienna, and were on their way to Paris.

When we boarded the bus, an American Express representative took the mic (always a bad sign on tours) and said she had some bad news for us. Their English-speaking driver and their tour guide had each met with similar but separate accidents the night before, and were not available to continue the trip.

Not to worry, she explained. A substitute driver had been located, and a new tour guide would join the bus in Paris. Until Paris, the tour would be without an English-speaking guide. She assured the group that they were in good hands.

At this point, our new driver, Udo, introduced himself and said, "I donn speak no good Ainglisch, thank you werry much." Not only were we without a guide, we were without an English-speaking driver. DOOM!

When the representative left the bus and the bus left the hotel, the psychologists and sociologists got from one another perfect lessons in social adulteration stratification and gestalt counseling. None of it worked and they were swinging from the luggage racks in ten miles.

I told Margie that I was "very uncomfortable" with this many uncomfortable educators, so I made my way up to the jump seat and asked Udo if he could understand my poor grade of Texas German. Strangely enough, I could understand him when he told me that he could understand me.

117

I asked him if it would be okay if I served as an interpreter for him and vise versa. When he agreed, I got on the horn and introduced myself to the group and tried to ease their minds about our dilemma. I offered to handle any emergency information and answer any travel questions. I explained to them that I had taught German history for a number of years and had written both my thesis and my dissertation on German subjects, and that I might be able to help pass along some helpful bits of information on the various historical sites we passed.

The perfect opportunity presented itself to get the collective mind of the group back to the trip as we approached Landsberg, just outside of Munich. This was the site of the prison where Hitler spent a brief vacation and wrote *Mein Kampff*. By the time we passed Landsberg, I had been elected tour guide.

Then we got to a small village on the outskirts of Memmingen, and a chorus went up for a potty stop and coffee. Udo demonstrated quite clearly that he was not used to tour groups. He stopped the bus at a small cafe in a typical little village (church, several house/barns, a store or two, all within a two-hundred yard radius).

One can imagine the consternation of the typical muscular German waitress (kellnerin) when she saw forty people come into her business. She spoke not one word of English but she directed people to the tables. It was pretty obvious that she intended to wait on one table at a time and we were going to be there until the next performance of the Oberammergau Passion Play.

At this point I asked her permission to have the people line up at the counter and let her wait on them one at a time. I acted as their interpreter and we made quick work of the task. As a reward, she condescended to speak with me (older German women would hardly ever speak to Americans.)

I asked her how long she had lived in the village. She said that she had lived there all her life. Sechsundsechsich jahren. Sixty-six years.

118

"In fact," she said, "I have never left the city. I have never been over the line marking the boundary to the city."

I could hardly believe this. Her whole life had been spent inside a two hundred yard circle.

Then she asked me where I lived. I told her in the USA.

"Where in the USA?" she asked.

"Texas."

"Really!" she exclaimed excitedly. "Kennen Sie J.R.?" ("Do you know J.R.?")

She immediately ran to the window and cried out to her husband who was working in the garden, "Come quickly. There is a man here who knows everything about Dallas."

Come to find out, she knew more about Dallas than I did. I never watched what I thought was a rather stupid presentation of our Texas way of life.

It amazed me that she could live her entire life in a small circle in a little village in south Germany (a land which she had not seen) and know so much about Dallas (which was really an illusion.) There is no end to the applications of the moral of that story.

## Lost Luggage in Erfurt

In 1984, as part of the special presentation of the Oberammergau Passion Play and the observance of the 500th anniversary of the birth of Martin Luther, we escorted a tour to Europe.

Everyone traveling behind the Iron Curtain retains certain memories and impressions which remain forever fixed. Our experiences produced these same permanent images which shall last forever (and certainly longer than did the Iron Curtain).

Our first night was spent in Frankfurt, and our first day of travel out of Frankfurt took us directly behind the Iron Curtain to Eisenach and Wartburg Castle (where Luther translated the New Testament into German). Then

119

we went directly to Erfurt and the incredible Cosmos Hotel.

The Cosmos Hotel was one of those showplaces which catered to tourists like ourselves and to Russian army officers from a divisional headquarters just a few kilometers away. It was the best hotel in town, but that was not saying a great deal. The Cosmos Hotel became the stage for the strangest scenario I ever witnessed.

If it were on Broadway, it would have been entitled, "Who Stole the Luggage?"

The worst of worst nightmares for a tour group has got to be lost luggage. When we were loading the bus in Frankfurt, it was there by the bus. When we unloaded at the Cosmos and went to our rooms, two suitcases were not in their customary places outside the room.

When the missing suitcases were reported to the desk, we discovered that hotel help in the German Democratic Republic were exclusively young, pale, thin high school girls. Somehow those little gals had managed to haul those suitcases to their appropriate places, and now they had the task of finding the lost articles.

Very efficiently they went to the sixth floor and started down. Result . . . no suitcases.

Perhaps we could call Frankfurt and see if the suitcases were still there?

Impossible. Rules would not permit this. It required twenty-four hours advance notice to get permission to call West Germany. We had to prove that they were not in the Cosmos Hotel.

Then came the hard part. If the suitcases were not in our rooms, and not in the halls, they could only be in the room of one of the Russian army officers. The thought scared those poor little German girls to death. But up they went to ask the officers for permission to search their rooms for two lost American suitcases.

In five minutes they returned pale, crying, shaking, and empty handed. It had obviously been an awful experience.

They decided that there was nothing to do but call the Vopos (Volkspolizei).

In ten minutes two characters appeared looking like they had been dressed by Charlie Chaplain and scripted by Peter Ustinoff. About every third step their shoulder straps would slip off of their shoulders.

Pitiful . . .

Their green hats had bills that looked like the caps of animal trainers in a Barnum and Bailey Circus act.

And attached to their sambrown belts were gas masks, of all things. Obviously they were not permitted to carry weapons, and it took something to make them look official.

They swaggered up to the desk and ask the Empfangsdamen (receptionist) what all the commotion was about, adding, "Wie koennen Sie dienen?" which is what waitresses ask customers in restaurants. The young lady explained to them that two American suitcases were missing.

"Well," they said, "Where are they?" Perfectly logical inquiry.

"If we knew that, we would not need you." Perfectly logical response.

Had we called Frankfurt to see if the bags were there? You know the response.

Then the two keystone cops were told that they must confront the Russian officers. This time they got pale, shaky, and sweating *before* they went upstairs. In ten minutes, back they came. Russian generals must really have a way of explaining things to German civil servants.

Then the call went out for Victor. Obviously an act of desperation. And in ten minutes, I saw why.

So help me, when Victor stepped through the door, everyone in the lobby shrank a little. They were all literally cowed by the presence of this man. And little wonder. Black Italian highheeled boots, black leather coat, Scottish tweeds, and a slick black hair cut in a 1960s ducktail. It would have been appropriate to sing the chorus from *Hello, Dolly*.

I fully expected to see him snap his fingers, but that was too much, I guess.

KGB!!!!!!

He heel clicked his way to the desk and said, "Tell me!"

And she did. Then it was his turn to ponder the incredible.

Victor turned to Joe Holt, our tour guide, and asked if Joe were certain the suitcase had gotten to the hotel. Joe, of course, said that he could not be certain.

Had we called the hotel in Frankfurt?

Joe answered that Victor knew this was not possible. (Wie Sie wissen, ich kann nicht das tun). One had to go to the police station and request a long distance line and then wait twenty-four hours, with little chance that permission would be granted to make the call.

Victor summed it up by saying that it was either call Frankfurt or go upstairs and face the Russians. He immediately reached for the phone, said a few things in Russian, and handed the receiver to Joe Holt.

"Here is your direct line to Frankfurt," he said.

Even the KGB did not want to mess with Russian officers.

Given the appropriate motivation, we can say to yonder mountain, "Be ye removed to the sea, and it shall be so . . ." even if we have to move it a rock at a time. Most of the barriers in the way of moving said mountain are those we voted into existence ourselves.

And most of the messes in which we find ourselves are the result of "We shalt not, saith man," rather than "Thou shalt not, saith the Lord."

By the way, the suitcases had been placed on the wrong bus in Frankfurt and ended up in Basel.

 ## Willing To Be Least

I was named president of East Texas Baptist College in April of 1976.

122

The first student I met as I left the board meeting after accepting this position was to set the tone for my relationship with hundreds of students who would follow.

Charles was a tall, slender, smiling, but melancholy young man. As I met him upon leaving Harvey Daniel Bruce Hall, I knew without anyone telling me that he was in the advanced stages of a crippling disease.

I soon learned, also without anyone telling me, that he had a radiant faith and a view of the world which was worth copying.

He experienced all of the inconveniences of a disease which attacks the connecting tissue of the body. He could not carry books and had to revert to the use of a satchel. He had numerous problems connected with mobility that would have stopped almost anyone from seriously seeking a college diploma. In particular, walking became increasingly difficult.

Charles did not actually walk. He simply took steps which required that he bring his leg into a circular sweep and place it in front of the stationary leg, and then he shifted his weight and began again the process in a countless series of painful maneuvers.

Nowhere was this more evident than on what must have been one of the finest days in his life — the day of graduation with his class.

The commencement ceremony was held in the sanctuary of First Baptist Church of Marshall. The platform and pulpit area were approachable from either side of the pulpit by steps which were, in fact, a stairwell. Therein lay the difficulty for Charles.

As he approached the stairwell to the platform, it became painfully clear to Charles, his classmates, platform guests, and some of the audience, that he could not swing his legs in a fashion that would be necessary for him to get up those steps. He could not go forward, he could not stay there, and he could not go back.

He knew it, the audience knew it, the graduates knew it.

It was one of those agonizing moments when everything is frozen in time.

Two people from the platform saw his dilemma and started toward Charles but he waved them off, as he did with offers of assistance from other students.

In an act of absolute courage, Charles reached down and gathered his robe around him, leaned forward, and eased himself up the steps on his knees.

THEN HE STOOD ERECT.

And when he stood, one thousand people in the audience stood with him. It was the most remarkable moment I have witnessed in over forty years of professional education. If the *Hallelujah Chorus* had not been written, someone would have penned it at that ceremony.

Charles then made his way, in that slow swinging gait, to the center of the stage to receive his diploma, holding out his hand in such a way that I could slide his diploma into his cupped fingers without embarrassment to him. Then came the AMEN to it all when he leaned close to me and said, "Dr. Dawson, isn't God good to us?"

I was absolutely certain as Charles made his way off stage that I had seen the perfect picture of a willingness to become least in the Kingdom and the resulting achievement of firstness in that same Kingdom.

## Allow The Children To Come To Me

I first knew Charles Wright when he was pastor at Manor and I was at McDade. He was working on a Master of Social Work, and I was in the Ph.D. program at the University of Texas.

On occasion we would car pool into Austin, which made for a great fellowship and a lasting friendship.

We both "left the ministry" about the same time, Charles going to Texas Baptist Children's Home in Round Rock and Dawson going to Wayland Baptist College in Plainview.

When Charles called me at Marshall and said that he

had a special burden to share with me, you can be sure that I listened very carefully.

Charles had several youngsters at the Children's Home who were approaching graduation and who truly needed to make a transition to college. But, as Charles so lovingly stated it, they needed a home, not just a campus.

It was pretty clear to both of us that we were talking about more than room and board, dorms and libraries . . . we were talking about assuming responsibility for brushing teeth and combing hair. And we were talking about money . . . a good deal of it.

I confessed to Charles that I had no earthly idea as to a source of support for the youngsters he had described, but I knew his heart, and was convinced that the Father would not have placed this burden on his heart without a plan to care for them.

We covenanted to make this an item of prayer. It was still on my heart when I got a call from Green Acres Baptist Church. My former pastor, Paul Powell, shared some news with me, and then asked if I had any prayer items he could share with his men. I responded with a recounting of my conversation with Charles. The prayer circle got bigger.

On Thursday, three days after my conversation with Charles and after numerous calls to prayer partners in East Texas, I received a call from an attorney for a Mrs. J. Rose, recently deceased after a long-time residence in the Nacogdoches area.

Mrs. Rose had provided in her will that after all of her burial costs were paid and several relatives were remembered, the residue of her estate, nearly $50,000, should be invested with the Baptist Foundation of Texas, with the income from the fund to be used to assist young people from Texas Baptist Children's Home who wanted to attend East Texas Baptist College.

She had written the will about the same time that the above-mentioned youngsters had entered Texas Baptist Children's Home. Through the many years in which these young folks had gone unvisited, unknown to relatives, and seemingly unloved by the world, Mrs. Rose cared for and prepared for an act of grace in the life of those she never saw in the flesh but loved in the spirit.

I think the Scriptures allude to a special kind of blessedness which accrues to those who, having not seen, believe anyway!!!

## Who Is My Neighbor, Lord?

Most people feel that they live in a pretty clearly defined area. The extent of their influence is generally felt to end at the city limits, the county line, or the Bureau of Vital Statistics.

Mrs. J. Rose probably lived a life pretty well defined as family boundaries. She most likely would have been astounded at the extent her influence has continued to be felt in the area of Christian ministry in Texas.

Shortly after learning that Mrs. Rose had specifically targeted Texas Baptist Children's Home as the beneficiary of her estate, I was overwhelmed by a sense of immediate need to visit Mr. and Mrs. A. E. (Earl) McGilberry of Shiro, Texas.

I had met Mr. McGilberry in a brief visit, through the friendship he had with Mac Runnels, development officer for many years at East Texas Baptist College. In October after coming to Marshall in August, I awoke one day with the feeling that I needed to make a visit to Shiro.

When I told Margie that I felt this unexplainable sense of direction about the visit, Margie reminded me that it was nearly three hundred miles to their home. It was going to be a long day. And when she asked why we were making the trip, I had to confess that I hadn't the faintest idea why I had the impulse to go.

After calling their home and receiving assurances that they would be open to a visit, we made our way to their home, all the while wondering just exactly what might transpire when we got there.

126

After exchanging pleasantries, Earl asked why I had come to see him, and suggested that it might be time for him to make a little contribution to a dormitory project we had just started . With that, he wrote me a modest check and I thanked him and prepared to leave, assuming that I had been "called" to Shiro for this purpose.

As we prepared to leave, I asked him about the home place of Guy and Ruby Foster. They had left an estate to benefit the eight colleges and universities related to the Baptist General Convention of Texas. The resulting scholarship programs held the possibility of helping untold thousands of students in the years to come.

Earl beamed at what I told him, explaining that they had neighbored with the Fosters for years, and that he and Guy had gone off to "the War" together in 1917. And he expressed surprise that their estate could benefit so many colleges.

More importantly, he was impressed by the immense effect the Fosters would have on future generations of young people.

His final word on the subject was, "That is interesting."

As we walked to the door, Geneva McGilberry came into the room. The only question she asked was, "Has anything interesting happened at the college recently?"

I answered her with a detailed account of Charles Wright's call for help on behalf of his students and the call from the attorney for Mrs. Rose. Her response to this miraculous turn of events was identical to that of her husband. "That is interesting," she said.

Two years later, Mrs. McGilberry called me to tell me that Earl had gone on to be with the Lord and reminded me that he had loved the college. Then she advised me to make a trip to the courthouse in Anderson, Texas to read Mr. McGilberry's will.

I did.

The day after our visit two years earlier, Earl had changed his will, duplicating the gift of his good friends Guy and Ruby Foster by naming the eight colleges of the

Baptist General Convention of Texas as beneficiaries of 1600 acres of land.

Then, even later, an attorney called to tell us that Mrs. McGilberry had joined her husband in glory, and shared with us that not one, but two wills had been changed that fateful day in October after we visited in their home. Following the lead of Mrs. J. Rose, and almost in the same mode as her husband, Mrs. McGilberry left over $600,000 in assets to Texas Baptist Children's Home.

I am told that this gift by this dear lady was the largest cash gift in the history of the Home.

The role I played in all of this was mainly that of a spectator, but I have never ceased to marvel at the ability of the Father to use good examples and good people to accomplish good things in His kingdom.

I also learned never to underestimate the eternal influence of good neighbors.

## Weimar and Buchenwald

The trip by my tour group behind the Iron Curtain in 1984 was pretty scary at times.

The harassment at border crossings, the bleakness of the cities, the sadness of the children, and the omnipresence of the Russian military made our visit a very somber experience. But the celebration of the 500th anniversary of Luther's birth created a brief openness that made the journey worthwhile.

It soon became apparent to all of us that the entire period in East Germany was a series of contradictions.

It was particularly emotional for me when I stood in the pulpit in Eisleben where Luther had preached his final sermon before being stricken. I have seldom experienced such a deep and moving sense of awe. Simply being there moved me as I have seldom been moved before or since.

Then we walked outside where we saw two children and an adult. The children seemed to be two of the saddest youngsters I have ever seen. It was in their eyes.

I asked the father, "Sie sind zehr Schade. Warum?" ("They are so sad. Why?")

It tore at my heart when he said, "Because they are here."

We experienced another classic contradiction when we approached a wheat field near the site of the famous Napoleonic Battle of Jena.

Our tour guide for our journeys in East Germany was Reines Barzuka, who was employed as a trumpet instructor at the university in Erfurt.

Little by little Rienes let us know of his work with evangelical youth choirs in the Erfurt area. And as he shared his remarkable faith which he could express only under the most difficult of circumstances, we came to appreciate him as a brother in Christ.

It took a while for him to come to the place where he trusted us to the point that he could openly proclaim his Christian faith. The main hindrance was his conviction that the tour bus was "bugged." It seemed like a terrible contradiction to talk about freedom in Christ when he could not freely talk about Christ.

When we approached the Napoleonic battlefield near Jena, he asked the driver to stop near a wheat field. There the contradiction between freedom and oppression was played out in the most touching and moving way.

We left the bus and walked into the field "white unto harvest."

When we were a safe distance from the bus, he shared the testimony of his faith with us. Then he opened an instrument case and took out his trumpet and played "Amazing Grace." The contradiction between the freedom of that wonderful song and the fear for his own safety fell heavily upon all of us.

This was especially evident when he said to us, "You Americans! All you want is UP and all we Germans want is OUT."

But the ultimate contradiction was that which we experienced at Buchenwald, site of one of the most infamous Nazi death camps.

As we stood at the monument marking the wanton extermination of a quarter of a million dreams, it struck me that this place marked the worst elements of humankind.

Then I heard the peeling of church bells off to the south of us and at the end of gently falling countryside. The eerie tones were evidently coming from churches in the direction of the classical city of Weimar.

The city of Weimar was the residence for the greatest minds of Germany during the Enlightenment. Any list of great contributors in poetry, literature, history, philosophy, and the arts reads like Weimar's city directory. When Germany tried to bring democracy into being after World War I, the choice for the seat of this dream was Weimar.

From Weimar you could see the gentle rise of the land ending with the ridge on which Buchenwald was located. From Buchenwald, the lowest point in German history, you could look down into the crucible of the greatest intellectual era in German history.

Man at his best and man at his worst stood at opposite ends of a gentle, neutral countryside. The terrible truth was that this classic contradiction of man's best and man's worst resides in each and every one of us.

God help us!!!

## Cannon . . . Or Was it Canon?

To visit the Swiss city of Zurich is to fall in love with it.

The Grossmuenster (cathedral) was the center of the Reformation in German-speaking Switzerland under Ulrich Zwingli. Lenin was in the city when the revolution erupted in Russia, and made his way to the Finland Station to initiate the Communism phase of the revolt. Goethe stayed there (along with ten thousand other locations in Europe).

First impressions are said to be the most lasting, and

the first thing I saw in this remarkable city was the Swiss National Museum which is located directly across from the train station. And the first thing I saw in this museum, built to represent a castle, was the cannon in the courtyard.

It was the most impressive cannon I have seen in all of Europe. It was a gift of Count Fusi to the canton for use in the war that resulted in the unification of the Swiss Confederation. (The term fusillade is derived from his name.)

I am a collector of noteworthy replicas of famous artillery pieces, and the sight of Count Fusi's cannon set my heart to shifting into high gear. I had to have a replica of that historic weapon. Surely, surely, I would find one for sale in the museum shop.

Wrong!

When I asked in my very best German if I could buy such a cannon, I was told, very politely, that such items were not sold there, and that they had no idea where one might be found.

The great adventure began at that point. Somewhere in Zurich I would find that elusive dream.

By late afternoon on that Saturday I found myself in an antique shop, knowing that time was running out. In those days shops closed at precisely 4:00 P.M. on Saturday in Zurich.

In desperation I repeated my question. "Do you know where I may purchase a small cannon like the large cannon in the courtyard of the Swiss National Museum (Schweizerisches Landesmuseum)?"

For the first time all day I got a different response. The clerk beamed and said, "Little cannons?" She raised a finger, pressed down, and said, "Boom, boom."

Yes!!!

"Go straight out the door, turn right and go one hundred meters, then left one hundred meters, then turn the corner and you will find the shop for cannons. But hurry, it is getting late." (Schnell. Du kommst spaet.)

I grabbed Margie, hurried out the door, followed the excellent set of directions and one minute before 4:00 P.M.,

131

turned the corner and looked into a camera shop, where they sold Canons.

I am certain that to this day there is a lady in Zurich who tells her German friends about this mixed-up American with the broken camera who thought he was asking for cameras when all along he was requesting cannons.

And Jesus said, "If you ask the Father for bread, will he give you a stone?"

## A Bowl of Corn Flakes

From the earliest days of my childhood one of the constant and unchanging memories was the picture of my father eating corn flakes (brand omitted as an act of kindness on my part.)

The last thing my father did before retiring for the night was to eat a bowl of corn flakes. Every morning his breakfast included a bowl of corn flakes.

Throughout the years of returning home for various special events and vacations, the one unchanging constant upon which I could depend to let me know I was home was that bowl of corn flakes before bed.

A month after my mother passed away, we returned home to help Poppa straighten the house and get everything in order. It dawned upon me that the folks who made my dad's favorite brand that had stood the test of five decades of devotion might like to hear about his brand loyalty. It just struck me as something they might like to know about.

So, when we got to the house, I went to the pantry to get a box of his corn flakes so that I might find an address to which I could send this wonderful story.

One can hardly imagine my shock at finding raisin bran, shredded wheat, and even corn puffs, but nary a box of corn flakes.

A little peeved that my father had ruined a perfectly good public relations story, I asked him what had happened to his favorite cereal.

132

His answer with simple. "Your mother always bought that. I never did really like that stuff."

Not surprisingly, I have heard people say the same thing about their years of church experiences. The only thing worse than an appetite managed by others is a spiritual appetite handled the same way.

This story may be a little humorous, but the sad fact is that when it comes to our walk with one another in the Kingdom Way, we are not much better about communicating some of our basic spiritual and human needs.

## Missions Begins At Home

Baptists are by nature devoted to the management style known as Management by Objective. We are constantly getting ready for the next big event. The Lottie Moon Christmas Offering for Foreign Missions, the next convention, the next revival, the next evangelism conference, the next high attendance Sunday, well, the list has no end to it.

If the Lord is planning the Rapture in the next year, the average Baptist is going to be pretty ticked off over someone "messing" with the annual calendar.

I was a victim of this on a mission trip to Stuttgart, Germany. International Baptist Church had extended an invitation to the Baptist General Convention to bring a retreat team to Stuttgart as a part of the Partnership Missions agreement we had with the European Baptist Convention.

I was privileged to have a leadership role in putting together the team of fifteen volunteers. Air reservations, local transportation, passports, daily assignments, prayer meetings, and other supporting meetings became "the" point of reference for everything else I had to do.

The critical moment for such ventures is always the day before departure time.

On that day I made the mistake of going through the offices of Mission Arlington at First Baptist Church. I say mistake, because I should have known I was destined to run into Tillie Bergin, and believe me, that is always a mistake.

When you are designing models for focus on a mission, draw a picture of this magnificent missionary who has worked a miracle in Arlington mission work.

You might think that Tillie might ask some type of question that would open the door for me to tell her about the big mission trip to Germany.

Not Tillie.

All she wanted was the name of a person I might know who could assume a leadership role in the puppet ministry for Mission Arlington.

I dodged the issue as best I could, and announced that I had big things in the making and I just did not have time to turn any attention to the puppet ministry of Mission Arlington. I then beat a hasty retreat before she convinced me to cancel my flight and immediately start the search for a leader for the puppet program.

The trip was all we had planned it to be, and more.

During a fellowship session at the retreat Larry Jones, pastor of International Baptist Church, announced that this was Reinhard Reschke's birthday and we should sing the American version of Happy Birthday to him.

Reinhard was a young baker who had just finished his apprenticeship training, and had become part of the IBC fellowship. He was a delightful person and I was immediately attracted to his smile and his obvious walk with his Savior.

I was also struck by his desire to learn English to a degree that he could qualify as a master baker. I was so moved by his ambition and his personality that I suggested that he should follow us back to the U.S. and enroll at the University of Texas in Arlington in their program of English as a Second Language. We offered him a bedroom at our home until he could feel comfortable to make the transition to dorm life on campus.

To make a long story short, in a miraculously short period of time he arrived in Arlington and was ready for his great adventure.

And almost as an after thought, it struck me that Reinhard might apply his baking skills by baking bread for Mission Arlington. Just a thought, mind you.

When I took him to Tillie's office for an appropriate introduction, the first question she asked was directed toward me, not Reinhard. And it was not a question. It was a demand.

"Where is my volunteer to help with the puppet ministry?"

To which Reinhard beamed and proudly announced, "I do puppets." He was a master puppeteer.

Silly me. All along I thought I was going to Stuttgart to be a missionary to them. In reality, I was going to Germany to fetch a man to come and do missionary work among us.

Reinhard finished his studies and is back in Germany, and is director of a full-time Christian puppet ministry. Mission Arlington is the better because he was here.

And I daily wonder what I may be missing while I am planning the next big event.

## On the Synagogue Search Committee

Sometimes Dawsonisms come back to haunt you.

My friend Evan was almost like a member of my family. His expertise in the travel business and my love for tours, trips, and mission teams made us both complementary and complimentary. Trust was earned, and was a coin commonly spent on behalf of one another's best interests.

On one occasion, and one only, Evan asked me to do something very nearly out of my realm.

He asked my help in securing a rabbi for the synagogue where he worshipped in Longview.

With slightly more than fifty family units, their appeal in securing leadership seemed pretty limited, but this did not prevent the search committee from seeking the most qualified man they could find.

Their search led them to a gentleman in Philadelphia who, at least on the surface, seemed over-qualified, for he

135

was a scribe as well as a rabbi, which entitled him to copy the Torah.

Evan said that the pivotal point in the offer they were making him was the fact that he held a Ph.D. in Educational Administration from the University of Alabama. Not shoddy credentials by any standard. An opportunity to teach on a limited basis at the graduate level just might be the enticement necessary to attract the man's interest.

This is were I came in. Evan wanted me to secure for the rabbi an interview at a regional university which might lead to his employment at the graduate level of instruction.

"C'mon, Dawson," he challenged. "Anybody who can get forty-five people in and out of East Germany without a hitch can pull that off."

I reminded him that we had lost Rusty Howell's luggage in Erfurt. It didn't phase him a bit.

In a word, this is how I ended up on the search committee for a rabbi for the synagogue in Longview.

The hard part came when I called a friend in Tyler to see if there might be a possibility for an opening in Education Administration for this rabbi I was trying to help get located in Longview.

Stony silence.

Then uproarious laughter.

"Dawson," he said. "I have heard a litany of absolutely unbelievable yarns, sheer fabrications, and pointless humor from you for years. I have laughed appropriately, believed blindly, and quoted faithfully . . . but you are NEVER going to make me believe that you are on a search committee for a rabbi."

Fortunately, an hour of sworn affidavits finally convinced him to really listen. The result was indeed an interview and beyond that the end result was the acceptance of the position at the synagogue by the rabbi.

Seems to me that the rabbi owes me a favor, but if you think my friend in Tyler was skeptical . . .

# ✗ Physician, Heal Thyself

Margie and I were attending a meeting of the Southern Association of Colleges and Schools in Atlanta when it occurred to us that we had not visited with our good friends — Buddy and Glenda Nail.

When we got together at a local restaurant it was immediately apparent that they had recently endured a profound life-threatening experience.

Glenda had found herself in a slow and ever-deepening downward health spiral. Over a period of months she had become increasingly weak and distressingly tired. Doctor after doctor had tried to diagnose her difficulties, but to no avail. The common thread that seem to run through it all was that she was obviously dying.

The last, final desperate effort at diagnosis and cure was to be exploratory brain surgery, and it was while she waited in the office of the surgeon that Glenda turned through the pages of a medical journal and came across an article on pernicious anemia.

As she read the article and ran down the list of symptoms, a light went on. Word for word, line for line, this article was an exact description of her physical condition.

When she was able to see the physician, Glenda showed him the article, and they both agreed that the recommended treatment — large doses of synthesized Vitamin B12 — was at least worth a try.

The end result of this decision was the restoration of her rapidly declining state of health. In a few months, despair for life turned into hope for tomorrow.

Then Buddy shared an unexpected twist to the story. In the more formal world of academe, Buddy was Dr. Billy Ray Nail, Vice President for Academic Affairs at a state school just outside of Atlanta.

His duties as dean, as well as his scientific interest as a math professor, led Buddy to a seminar hosted by the Chemistry Department.

One can almost imagine the overflowing of feelings he

experienced when the speaker was introduced as the key member of the scientific group credited with the synthesis of Vitamin B12. Here was the man responsible for saving Glenda's life.

To say that he was "deeply moved" would most certainly be an understatement. According to Buddy, he waited until the crowds had departed after the chemist's lecture, and then he made his way to the lectern and tried to find some adequate means to express the gratitude he felt toward this scientist he had just met, but to whom he owed so much.

The scientist listened patiently as Buddy told him of the months of agony and fear and the desperate search for an appropriate diagnosis of his wife's symptoms.

Buddy noticed that his listener suddenly became incredibly pale. The man was absolutely transfixed as Buddy told him of the treatment with this man's own chemical creation.

Then the man almost shouted, "SIR, YOU HAVE JUST DESCRIBED MY WIFE'S PHYSICAL CONDITION!!!"

As incredible as it seems, the wife of the scientist was dying for want of the very substance her own husband had discovered.

In the afterglow of the good endings to two similar stories, I could hardly keep from noting that the presence of a cure for spiritual problems in the form of Jesus Christ is no guarantee that the appropriate application will be made, even by those who are in the greatest need.

##  Enemies of the Cross of Christ

The year 1994 proved to be a pretty nostalgic year for students of World War II.

The world became absolutely captivated by the retelling, in the most minute detail, of the events which led to the Normandy invasion and the beginning of the end of this terrible ordeal.

Like most trained historians, I became emotionally and personally involved with the magnitude and depth of change this terrible war brought to bear on so many millions of lives.

When I agreed to assist in a Partnership Missions trip to Estonia in April of 1994, I had no way of knowing that missions, tragedy, war, victory, and the resurrection would all come together for me when I had the chance to see the end of a fifty year story.

Our visit to Estonia took us first to Tallinn and the offices of Estonian Baptist work. Then a short trip took us to Parnu. All trips in Estonia are short. The whole country covers about six Texas counties.

We were guests of Joseph and Aime Tommu, in one of the oldest and finest Baptist churches in Parnu, and I was honored to have the privilege of speaking to the most beautiful and courageous people I have ever known. As they shared their stories of hardship and suffering under the Communist regime, I felt an enormous sense of indebtedness to them. Somehow it seemed they had done all of this for me, as well as for their Lord.

As the conclusion of the services, Joseph took us to Salem Baptist Church, and as we stood in front of that church, he recounted an amazing story.

Germany and Russia signed an infamous agreement on August 23, 1939 by which Hitler granted to Russia the "right" to Estonia. Shortly thereafter, Red Army forces moved into bases in tiny Estonia and the horrible nightmare began.

One of the most terrible results of the occupation was the massive deportations of thousands of Estonians to Russia — most of whom never have returned and never shall. Parnu was especially devastated by the deportations and by the accompanying imprisonments and executions among the tiny population of this very small country.

The assault upon the population was made even worse by the assault upon the intellect of the remaining citizens. The Estonian language was banned, books were confiscated, schools "re-educated" around Communist dictums.

Added to this was the assault upon the spirit of the

people. All teaching in the churches was banned. Evangelism was prohibited.

And, finally, churches were confiscated and given over to demeaning uses by the Communist regime. This was the fate of Salem Church.

On the front of the church was a cross of wood inlaid in the stone wall of the church. Since digging the wood out of the stone would accomplish little except leave another form of the cross intact, they decided to cover the entire cross with a symbol of the Communist Youth League, who occupied the gymnasium which had been installed in the sanctuary of the church.

Deportations, executions, and fifty-one years took their toll, and Salem Church slowly vanished from the conscious memories of its surviving people.

Then came the magnificent swell of freedom in 1991, when the proud people of Estonia marched to the Toompera in Tallinn and told the Russians to pack it up and get out of Estonia — the first liberated people to ask the Russians to go home.

Almost immediately, some of the older saints in Parnu went to the city council and asked for immediate return to their rightful owners a number of public buildings in the city which had been confiscated and held for more than fifty years.

But who were the rightful owners? Records were gone. After all, under communism you had no "ownership." Give us something to prove the claims and we will consider the request, said the council.

Then came an act of enormous faith. If they could not prove ownership and get the church back, at least they could take down that awful symbol of the Communist Youth League on the front of the building.

So, up went the ladders, out came the crowbars, down came the symbol of tyranny.

AND THERE IT WAS . . . THE CROSS!!!

It had been there all along, waiting to be revealed.

Needless to say, as we entered Salem Baptist Church, I knew we were walking on holy ground. It almost became shouting ground when the pastor celebrated the moment in a Bible study by recalling the words of Paul to the church at Philippi.

"He who begun a good work in you is able to finish it unto the day of Christ Jesus." *(Phil. 1:6)*

Three months after this inspiring moment in Parnu, we were concluding services at the Summer Assembly of the European Baptist Convention at Interlaken, Switzerland.

I had shared with these wonderful folks from all over Europe the story about Salem Baptist Church and the wonderful and victorious conclusion to more than fifty years of anguish and pain.

At the conclusion of the service, a couple approached us. He was of that marvelous tall, straight, intense breed of folks from Estonia.

He finished the story about Parnu.

His father had been one of those thousands of innocent folks from Parnu who were deported to Russia. But the ship carrying the victims never left the harbor. It detonated a mine and exploded, throwing him overboard.

He swam to shore and made his way to his home. Knowing his life was forever in peril in Estonia, he fled the country with his wife and children and made their way eventually to Switzerland.

The parents are now gone, but the son seemed to finish the saga when he said, "My father always wondered whatever happened to the Salem Church in Parnu."

Then his eyes looked far away.

"He knows, doesn't he?"

Then he turned and walked away.